Foundation Flex for Designers

Greg Goralski

LordAlex Leon

friendsof ™

DESIGNER TO DESIGNER™

an Apress® company

Foundation Flex for Designers

Credits

Lead Editors
Chris Mills, Ben Renow-Clarke

Technical Reviewer
Mike Jones

Editorial Board
Steve Anglin, Ewan Buckingham, Tony Campbell, Gary Cornell, Jonathan Gennick, Jason Gilmore, Kevin Goff, Jonathan Hassell, Matthew Moodie, Joseph Ottinger, Jeffrey Pepper, Ben Renow-Clarke, Dominic Shakeshaft, Matt Wade, Tom Welsh

Project Manager
Beth Christmas

Copy Editor
Liz Welch

Associate Production Director
Kari Brooks-Copony

Production Editor
Ellie Fountain

Compositor
Lynn L'Heureux

Proofreader
April Eddy

Indexer
Brenda Miller

Cover Image Designer
Corné van Dooren

Interior and Cover Designer
Kurt Krames

Manufacturing Director
Tom Debolski

CONTENTS AT A GLANCE

CONTENTS

ABOUT THE AUTHORS

Greg Goralski is an interdisciplinary interactive designer based in Toronto. He is an alumni of the Canadian Film Centre Media Lab and the Interactive Project Lab. He has won Gold at the National Post Design Exchange awards and has presented his work at numerous festivals, including the World Expo in Aichi, Japan. As a professor at the Humber College School of Media Studies, he divides his time among playing with technology, training the next generation of interactive designers, and being inspired by his students. Greg also drinks too much coffee, and should really be living on a beach. His website is www. greggoralski.com.

LordAlex Leon is an active member of the Flash community and a well-respected industry leader with over 7 years of experience creating content and applications for the Internet and devices. He is the founder of LordAlex Works™ (LAW), a Flash platform consultancy firm based in Montreal, Quebec, Canada, helping new media and content providers deliver intelligent, rich Internet content and powerful applications based on the Flash platform.

LordAlex runs a personal blog dedicated to the Flash platform and related technologies that you can read at www.lordalex.org.

You can find LordAlex in his spare time writing tutorials in English, French, and Spanish or speaking at international events and conferences. LordAlex also runs the local official Montreal Adobe User Group, the largest AUG in the province of Quebec.

ABOUT THE TECHNICAL REVIEWER

Mike Jones is an old man of the Flash world, having first picked up Flash in late 1996, when it was still called Futurewave Splash. For over a decade now, he has produced web applications, websites, and desktop applications, all developed using the Flash platform—not once thinking that perhaps it was time to find something better to do.

In his spare time, Mike runs the website FlashGen.com (www.flashgen.com). Originally launched as a Macromedia Generator resource site in 1998, Mike now uses it as a blog-style repository for information based on Flash, Flex, AIR, and ActionScript. He lives in Haslemere, Surrey, UK, with his fiancée and their cat, Figo.

ABOUT THE COVER IMAGE DESIGNER

Corné van Dooren designed the front cover image for this book. After taking a brief break from friends of ED to create a new design for the *Foundation* series, he worked at combining technological and organic forms, with the results now appearing on this and other books' covers.

Corné spent his childhood drawing on everything at hand and then began exploring the infinite world of multimedia—and his journey of discovery hasn't stopped since. His mantra has always been "The only limit to multimedia is the imagination," a saying that keeps him moving forward constantly.

Corné works for many international clients, writes features for multimedia magazines, reviews and tests software, authors multimedia studies, and works on many other friends of ED books. You can see more of his work at and contact him through his website, www.cornevandooren.com.

If you like Corné's work, be sure to check out his chapter in *New Masters of Photoshop: Volume 2* (friends of ED, 2004).

ACKNOWLEDGMENTS

I would like to thank Maclin Williams and Mark Okon for the use of their photos and animations. These wonderful visuals helped us greatly. I would also like to thank the 2008 graduating class of Multimedia at Humber College who served as the test bed for some of these projects and gave us invaluable insight.

Greg Goralski

Special thanks to Tom Green for his sound advice; to Matt Chottin, Ted Patrick, and Mike Jones for their help in dealing with some of the difficult parts of this book; to my coauthor Greg Goralski, whose dedication and perseverance were an inspiration for me while creating this book; and last but not least to friends of ED for making this book a reality.

LordAlex Leon

INTRODUCTION

Welcome to *Foundation Flex for Designers*. When Adobe released Flex 1.0 in March 2004, a lot of designers and developers who were used to working in Flash viewed it with suspicion. Where was the timeline, what was MXML, and how was it useful for designers? With Flex 2, the answers to those questions became a little clearer, and more and more web developers started to pick up Flex. With the release of Flex 3, it's clear that Flex is now *the* tool for rich Internet application (RIA) development. It's easy for developers to pick up and rapidly create RIAs, and there's now more customizability available for designers to sink their teeth into.

This book deals with the designer issues of creating RIAs in Flex Builder 3. It covers such important issues as how to control the look and feel of an application through CSS and custom skins. It also shows how you can create these skins using the familiar tools of Photoshop, Illustrator, and Flash, rather than having to struggle to learn a new interface. The book also explores using transitions and other effects to make applications more dynamic, visually interesting, and easier to navigate.

Don't worry, though—we're not here to blind you with science and turn you into hard-core coders. You'll have to be familiar with a little bit of code to get the most out of Flex, but we're here to help, and we'll make sure that all the code is supplied for you so you can get on with the design. If, however, you want to delve a little deeper into the code, there are parts of the book where you can do just that and learn how to add complex functionality to your designs. If you want to go further still, we'll recommend the best places to get that information.

We're happy to have you along for this ride, and we hope you enjoy it and learn a lot from it. Flex isn't just for programmers; it's time for designers to take back RIAs, and show what that "R" really stands for. The Internet is not just about collecting data; it's also about visual communication and giving people a rich user experience, and that's what designers do best.

Layout conventions

To keep this book as clear and easy to follow as possible, the following text conventions are used throughout.

Important words or concepts are normally highlighted on the first appearance in **bold type**.

Code is presented in `fixed-width` font.

New or changed code is normally presented in **`bold fixed-width font`**.

Pseudo-code and variable input are written in *`italic fixed-width font`*.

Menu commands are written in the form Menu ➤ Submenu ➤ Submenu.

Where I want to draw your attention to something, I've highlighted it like this:

> *Ahem, don't say I didn't warn you.*

Sometimes code won't fit on a single line in a book. Where this happens, I use an arrow like this: ➡.

```
This is a very, very long section of code that should be written all ➡
on the same line without a break.
```

Chapter 1

INTRODUCING FLEX AND FLEX BUILDER 3

What we'll cover in this chapter:

- Flex Builder interface
- Using layout components
- Using control components
- Liquid design layout

Files used in this chapter:

- Completed example archive: Chapter1-completedExample.zip
- Chapter1Code.rtf

Let's start by having a look at where Flex fits into the bigger picture and then work our way deeper. Flex is a part of what is being referred to now as the Adobe Flash Platform. The Flash Platform is a family of tools that allow for the kind of dynamic interactivity that we have become familiar with through flash websites in a variety of uses. This includes Flash Lite, for mobile applications on cell phones and PDAs; Flash, the dominant tool for highly interactive websites; Flex, specialized for rich Internet applications; and AIR, for desktop applications. Each of these tools has a specialized purpose or environment of use, but all have the same technology under the hood, specifically the programming language ActionScript.

Together these tools allow you to create interactive sites or applications that can run off a cell phone, a web server, or your computer desktop and that have consistent interactivity without page reloads.

Rich Internet applications

Of these different environments, Flex is aimed at creating rich Internet applications, also called rich media web applications. These applications are similar to websites except that they offer more functionality than a traditional website. For example, a web page that shows a list of cell phones you can buy can best be called a website and should be built in Flash or HTML. A web page that allows you to organize that list by price and functions and then lets you order the one you want can best be described as a rich Internet application.

It is true that Flash allows you to create this web application, but it would involve creating much of it from scratch, taking a very long time and eating up a large budget. Flex uses prebuilt objects that can be modified or used as they are to make this kind of more complex application faster and cheaper. The prebuilt objects are part of the Flex framework, a collection of code libraries and application services that make development easier. These services include data-binding tools, drag-and-drop management, and visual effects, among others.

The use of prebuilt objects makes a big difference in the kinds of projects a team can create and the kinds of production processes that come into play.

Creating your first project

The first project that we will be building is a simple web feed reader, just to give you a taste of what the Flex workflow is like. If you're not already familiar with it, a web feed reader is a program that can read and present the content of web feeds such as blogs within your site. A web feed is essentially an XML file that contains the content from the blog you are viewing. You can see an example of the finished web feed reader at http://lordalex.org/flex4designers/atomreader/AtomReader2.html.

Once you install and open Flex, you should see a variety of panels, with the most prominent being the Flex Start Page, as shown in Figure 1-1.

The Flex Start Page gives you quick access to tutorials and example files that come with Flex Builder 3. These are very useful and we will begin using them in the second chapter. For now, let's create a new project so that we can have a look into the interface in development mode.

As you go to create a new project, you will find that you have more options than with most programs. This is your first hint that Flex can be a pretty powerful tool.

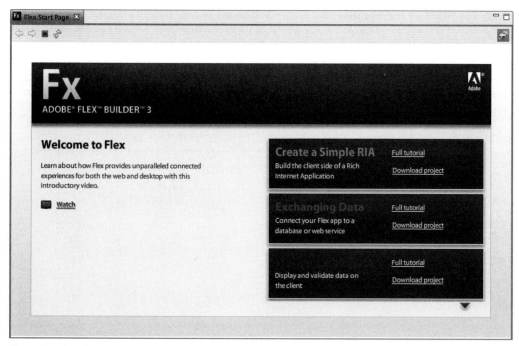

Figure 1-1. The Flex Start Page

1. Select File ➤ New ➤ Flex Project to create a new project, as shown in Figure 1-2.

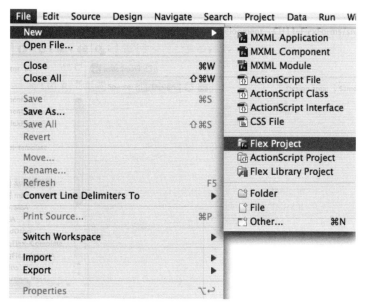

Figure 1-2. Creating a new project

2. The New Flex Project dialog box (Figure 1-3) allows you to name the project and define any server technologies that you may want to use. For our examples, we will be using XML, which does not need a specific server definition. Name the project atomReader.

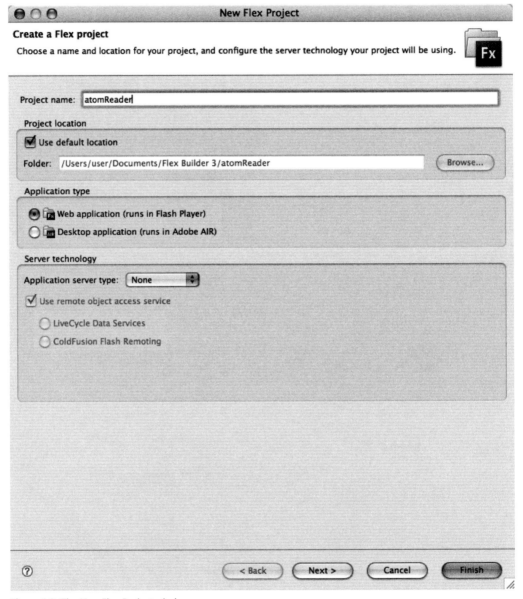

Figure 1-3. The New Flex Project window

In this dialog box (see Figure 1-4), you can also set project type to be a web or desktop (AIR) application.

3. Note the location of the project. This location is where all the files associated with the project will be created, and it will be important later when you'll place additional files in the folder. Click Finish to create the project.

Figure 1-4. Note the location of the project.

The Flex Builder 3 interface

Let's have a look around to see what is familiar and what is different from the tools you may have used before (see Figure 1-5). The Flex interface will look somewhat familiar to those who are used to working with Dreamweaver (for example, the ability to jump between Design and Source views) and also to those who are used to working in Flash (such as the row of components along the left). The interface may also feel strange at the start. The Flex properties, for instance, are distinct from other programs. Probably most designers will be wondering, "Where are my drawing tools?" The answer is "Gone," but don't worry—Flex plays very nicely with other software that's specialized for developing graphics. We will be looking at how Flex works with Fireworks in Chapter 4, and how it works with Photoshop and Illustrator in Chapter 5.

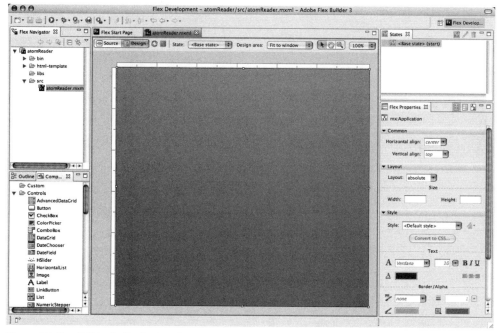

Figure 1-5. Flex Builder in the Design view

The first interface part affected is the Navigator panel, which is at the top left of the screen. Notice that in this panel we have our project name along with a couple of folders that Flex Builder created for us.

The most important file here is atomReader.mxml. This file holds the main layout and design information for our project, and can be considered similar to the index.html file in an HTML project. Your main area within the center holds the MXML Editor (see Figure 1-6). This area shows the code of the MXML file when Source is selected and a visual representation of the MXML file when Design is selected. In this Design view, you can also drag and drop components. Let's give that a shot now.

Figure 1-6. The MXML Editor

A first look at Flex components

Designing in Flex is much more about using prebuilt components that get modified and customized than starting from scratch every time. This is how Flex allows you to create sophisticated applications more quickly and easily than you normally would be able to within other programs. It also gives you the tools to customize the look, movement, and interaction of the components to create creative personalized interfaces. These components can be found in the Components panel (see Figure 1-7).

The first thing that you should notice is that there are a heck of a lot of them. The reason for this is because they can do a lot of the heavy lifting when it comes to building applications, and they can cover most application needs. They are used to control the layout, as with a panel, or interactions, as with buttons, or control navigation, as with a tabbed menu system.

Figure 1-7. The Components panel

4. Our first component is the Panel component. You can find it in the Layout folder in the Components panel. Drag and drop the Panel component into the MXML Editor, and it should wind up looking something like Figure 1-8.

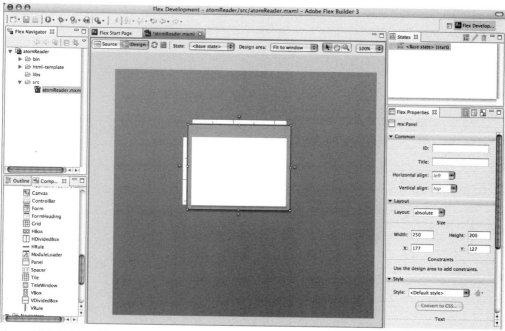

Figure 1-8. Interface with the Panel component in the MXML Editor

This is a good time to have a look at what MXML is exactly and what dragging a component into the MXML Editor does. There are two ways of looking at the application that is laid out in MXML. Figure 1-8 shows how the Panel component looks in the Design view.

5. If you switch to the Source view (see Figure 1-9), you can see the underlying code that is created for the application.

Figure 1-9. Moving from Design to Source view

You can see this code in Figure 1-10. The code's structure is similar to XML because MXML is an XML-based language, and you use the MXML code to lay out user-interface components for your applications. The first line defines the version of XML used. The second line defines the application, and it is inside these application tags that we place our components. You can see that within the application tags we now have the tags for the Panel component that we created in the Design view. The Panel tags start with <mx:Panel. . .>, which contains the properties of the component, and end with </mx:Panel>. So far, the properties are the default size and location that occurred when we created the component. You may also have noticed that the interface changed when we made the transition to Source view. This is because working within the Source view is significantly different than working in the Design view. We no longer have the Components panel visible. This is because in the Source view, you can write the components in directly by typing the MXML tags. Similarly, the Properties panel also disappears because we can write the properties directly into the tags. This way of working is often more comfortable for developers. The MXML tag calls on a large amount of ActionScript that makes the component possible and functional. This all happens in the background, so we do not have to worry about that ActionScript; we just have to worry about the settings.

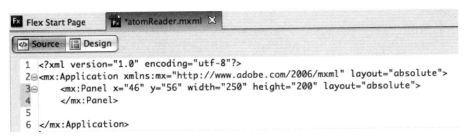

Figure 1-10. The MXML source for the panel

6. Jumping back to the Design view we can see again how this component will look to the user. Along the right, you will find the Properties panel (see Figure 1-11.)

The Properties panel allows you to control things about the component such as size, name, colors, and layout. We will be looking into how to use these to control the look and reaction of the components in future chapters. For now, let's give this panel an ID of mainPanel, which allows us to call on it in the future, and a title. The ID is similar to an instance name in Flash, and the Title is similar to a label. For the Title, type Easy Atom Reader (see Figure 1-12.)

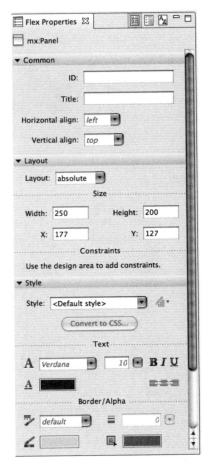

Figure 1-11. The component's Properties panel

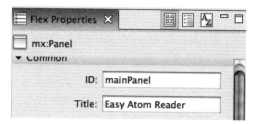

Figure 1-12. Panel's ID and Title

Flex fluid layouts

We are going to do one more thing with this panel that Flex is very good at: making the design fluid. By this I mean that when the size of the browser is adjusted, the content adjusts to use all the available space. You can do this by setting the size of your panel not by its width and height but by its distance from the edges.

Scrolling down through the Properties panel, you will find the layout options (see Figure 1-13).

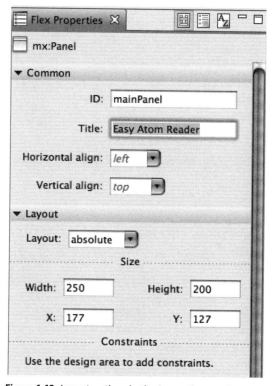

Figure 1-13. Layout options in the Properties panel

7. The panel component has a series of four layout handles. Each of these can be set to anchor, unanchored, or center. By setting them to anchor, the component is scaled until it is a set number of pixels from the edge of the application or the component it is nested in. Setting a layout handle to be anchored also produces a field within the layout properties for the component that lets you set the number of pixels from the edge of the application you want the component to be anchored. Set each of the four layout handles to anchor and set the value of each to 20 px (see Figure 1-14). This gives a gutter of 20 pixels.

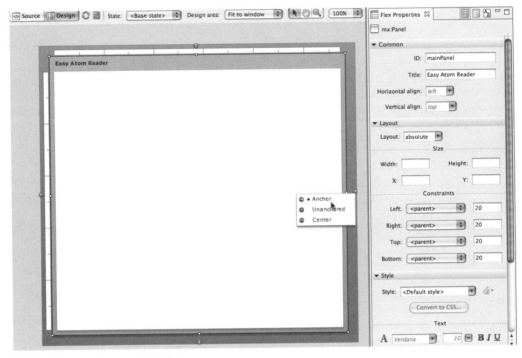

Figure 1-14. Apply these layout settings.

8. Test the application at this stage by selecting Run from the menu (you can also click the green play button). This will open your project in your default browser.

9. Play with the size of the browser to see how the fluid design works.

Displaying content

The white area of the panel is the content area, so next we need to put what kind of content we want in it. Since RSS feeds are text, we want to put in a text area. You can find the TextArea component in the Controls folder of the Component panel.

10. Drag and drop a TextArea component onto the white area of the panel; it is placed inside the panel content area and so will be adjusted with the panel (see Figure 1-15).

11. Move the TextArea component to the top-left corner of the panel, and by grabbing the bottom-right corner, stretch it out to fill the entire white area of the panel, as shown in Figure 1-16.

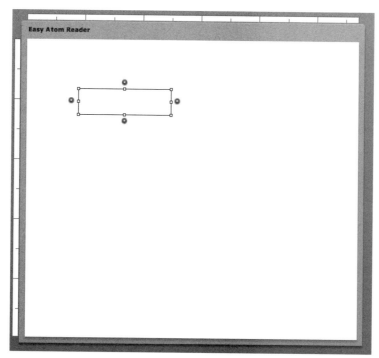

Figure 1-15. The TextArea component on the panel

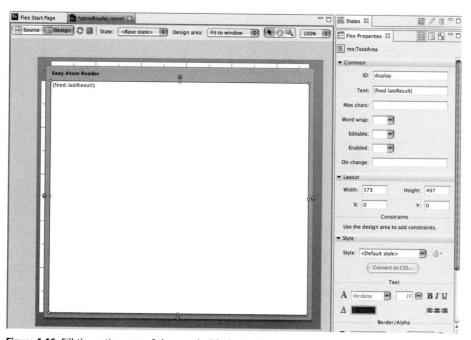

Figure 1-16. Fill the entire area of the panel with the TextArea component.

12. Give the TextArea component an ID of display (note the ID field of the Properties panel in Figure 1-16).

13. In the Text field of the Properties panel, set the text field to {feed.lastResult} (see the Text field in Figure 1-16).

Soon we will be setting up the feed, and this text will let it know what part of the feed to put into this text area.

14. Set the layout handles for the text area to be anchor, as shown in Figure 1-17. This will cause the text area to fill the entire panel content area regardless of the size of the browser window.

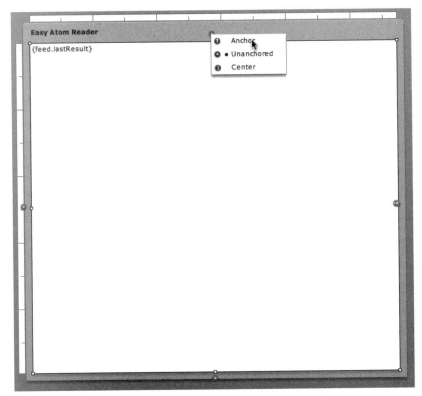

Figure 1-17. The layout constraints of TextArea

15. Next let's put a ControlBar layout component along the bottom of the panel, using drag and drop as we did before, as shown in Figure 1-18. You can change the height of the control bar by changing its layout properties; 50 is a good number for the height value.

In a panel, the content can change based on the interaction with the user. A ControlBar lets you keep some elements on the panel consistent. Generally, these are the buttons and other components that control the content.

16. On the ControlBar, place a TextInput by dragging it from the Controls folder in the Components panel—see Figure 1-19 in the next section. This is the area that will hold the URL of the web feed that we want to bring in, as you'll see in a moment.

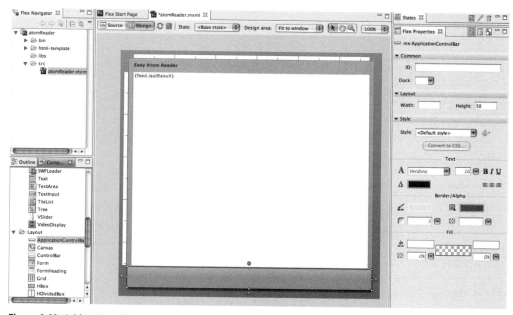

Figure 1-18. Add a ControlBar component.

Pulling in web feeds to Flex

Now we'll load and display the contents of a web feed in our Flex application—we're talking about the kinds of feed you see on blogs, news sites, and so forth. We will be using an Atom feed, located at http://www.lordalex.org/atom.xml, for the default feed to display. Atom is the format that is used by Blogger.com, and is in competition with other formats such as RSS 1.1 and RSS 2.0. Each of the formats is just a different way of representing the XML that has the text of the web feed. Since each format structures the XML in a different way, each would need to be processed differently, which would require a good deal of ActionScript. To keep this exercise focused on what is important to designers, working with components to lay out an application, we have decided to stick to just this one format.

17. Place the URL of the feed in the text property of the TextInput component. We will be able to change this directly within the site to pull in different feeds during runtime. We also need to put in an ID for this component to allow us to manipulate it later with code.

18. Give the TextInput an ID of urlFeed, and enter http://www.lordalex.org/atom.xml as the Text. The TextInput will adjust its size to suit the text, or you can stretch it to a size you prefer (see Figure 1-19).

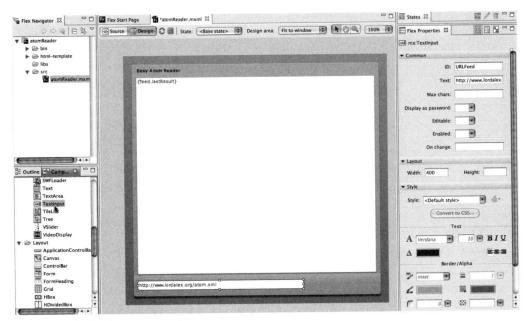

Figure 1-19. The TextArea component

Now we need a Button to trigger things; it is the first of the components in the Controls folder.

19. Place the Button next to the TextInput on the controlBar, in the same manner as before, as shown in Figure 1-20.

20. Give this button a label of Load Feed. Although it is not absolutely necessary to give an ID to this button, it is good practice to always provide an ID. Enter loadButton as the ID.

21. The property that tells us what the button will do when it is clicked is rather logically called On click. Enter feed.send() for its value (note this in the Properties panel in Figure 1-20.) This will send the URL in the inputText as the location of our feed. This allows us to change that URL at any point within the website.

Now we just need to create the feed. Normally this would require quite a bit of coding, but we will use a very direct simple method to bring in the feed called the HTTPService tag.

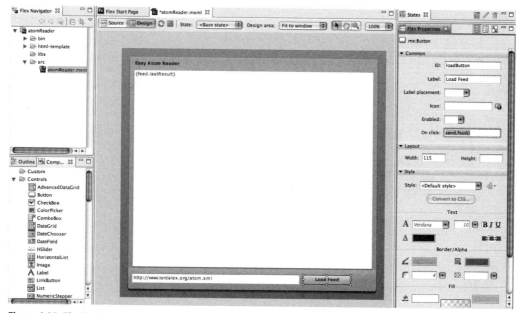

Figure 1-20. The Button component

22. Jump over to the Source view, as you'll need to type this code in. Take a moment to see what the MXML code looks like for our project so far—see Figure 1-21.

```
1  <?xml version="1.0" encoding="utf-8"?>
2  <mx:Application xmlns:mx="http://www.adobe.com/2006/mxml" layout="absolute">
3      <mx:Panel layout="absolute" left="10" right="10" top="10" bottom="10" id="mainPanel" title="Easy Atom Reader">
4          <mx:TextArea x="0" y="0" width="431" height="447"/>
5          <mx:TextArea id="display" text="{feed.lastResult}" left="0" right="0" top="0" bottom="0"/>
6          <mx:ControlBar height="50" y="408">
7              <mx:TextInput id="urlFeed" text="http://www.lordalex.org/atom.xml " width="306"/>
8              <mx:Button label="Load Feed" id="loadButton" click="feed.send()"/>
9          </mx:ControlBar>
10     </mx:Panel>
11  </mx:Application>
```

Figure 1-21. The source MXML

You can see that each of our components is represented here as tag similar to XML. These tags carry the same information that we set for our components in the Design view, and each of these properties can be modified here. We will be adding the line of code shown in Figure 1-22 before line 3.

```
<mx:HTTPService id="feed" url="{urlFeed.text}" resultFormat="e4x"/>
```

Figure 1-22. The HTTPService tag

Let's break this line up so that we can see what it does. First we have the HTTPService identified and named with the id, feed. Notice that this is the name of the feed that we have been using with the other components that work with this feed. For example, the TextInput has {feed.lastResult} and our button has feed.send(). The next piece of code, url ="{urlFeed.text}", tells the HTTPService to look into our inputText component (which we called urlFeed) for the location of the feed. The final piece of code, resultFormat="e4x", defines the structure that the information gets pulled into. This is more of a developer topic, but ECMAScript for XML (E4X) can also be very useful for designers as it is a new way to bring in XML data in a more intuitive way. The result ="onResult(event)" defines when the feed is called.

> Traditionally, bringing in XML data has involved a complex series of loops that organize the data. With the E4X method, you can call on a piece of information using the name and location it has within the XML file. For example, if you want to call on the title of the third post in your file, you can find it at xmlData[3].title. This is a good deal easier than past methods.

23. Add this line of code now.

24. Let's have a look at what we have created so far. Select Run ➤ Run atomReader, as shown in Figure 1-23.

Figure 1-23. Choose Run atomReader from the Run menu.

> You can find a completed version of this project at this stage in the folder atomReader1 *in the code download for this book at* www.friendsofed.com.

The current project output will look like Figure 1-24.

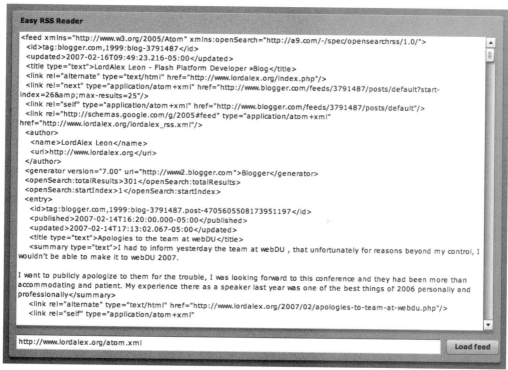

Figure 1-24. Atom Reader with unparsed text

Sources of feeds and limitations

Since this Atom Reader is looking directly at the XML file that creates this particular blog, to open a different blog you will need to point directly to its XML file. Most of the time this is as simple as adding /atom.xml to the URL. So for example, instead of typing http://www.myBlog.com, you enter http://www.myBlog.com/atom.xml.

There are some situations where this will not work. If the blog uses a different format, as mentioned before, such as RSS 2.0, it will not display. It is also possible that the person setting up the blog placed the atom.xml file in a location other than the default location, preventing our reader from finding it. There is one more reason for a blog not to work. For Flex or Flash to accept a feed from a different site, that site must have a crossdomain.xml file. This is a small file that sits on the server and gives permission to the Flex or Flash file to access it. This is done for security reasons and most blogs have the file. It is possible to make this reader more robust and take into account these possibilities, but it would require a good deal of ActionScript. Rather than make this chapter into a coding exercise, we have decided to keep the technique simple, even if it won't always work.

Formatting the feed

You will notice that the text looks a bit messy. That is because we just loaded the XML file as is. This is how the XML file looks like by default, without any formatting or organization being applied to it. The organization of an XML file is known as *parsing* and involves placing each part of the XML file into a variable. To parse and format the XML, we need to get into the nitty-gritty and manipulate the XML through ActionScript. This is getting into developer territory a bit, so we have provided the code. It can be found in the Chapter 1 folder of the book's code download, available on www.friendsofed.com. The file is called RSSFormattingCode.txt. Although this is code that would normally be created by your developer, it is interesting to have a look at it, especially if you are the kind of designer who also works with code.

25. Copy the code from the text file into your project in the Source view, above the HTTPService line we just added, as shown in Figure 1-25. Any script that you place in the MXML goes inside of `<mx:script></mx:script>` tags.

The file with the full script can be found in Chapter1Code.rtf in the code download for this book.

In a nutshell, what this code does is take the information coming in from the feed, pull out the pieces that it wants (specifically the title and summary), and stitch them together within a text variable, adding some text formatting along the way.

Let's break it out a bit further. The entire ActionScript is contained within the `<mx:Script>` tags; this helps keep the code organized and separated from the MXML. We create an array called xmlData, which holds all of our entries, and then create a for loop that pulls the title and summary of each post into variables called currTitle and currSummary. The text in these two variables then get stitched together and placed into the variable currPost. When we are stitching them together, we add `<strong>` tags around the title to make the title bold, and \n\n tags to give us line breaks between the title and summary. The next piece adds the recently stitched post to any previous posts that have already been stitched. The final bit of code places the final long piece of text into our display text area as HTML text.

Source Design

```
1   <?xml version="1.0" encoding="utf-8"?>
2   <mx:Application xmlns:mx="http://www.adobe.com/2006/mxml" layout="absolute">
3   <mx:Script>
4       <![CDATA[
5
6           //Import statements
7           import mx.rpc.events.ResultEvent;
8
9           //Namespaces declaration
10          namespace atom = "http://www.w3.org/2005/Atom";
11          namespace openSearch = "http://a9.com/-/spec/opensearchrss/1.0/";
12          namespace feedburner = "http://rssnamespace.org/feedburner/ext/1.0";
13
14          //Public variables
15          public var xmlData:XMLList;
16
17          //Parse the data coming from atom feed
18          private function onResult( event:ResultEvent ):void
19          {
20              //Open namespaces
21              use namespace atom;
22              use namespace openSearch;
23              use namespace feedburner;
24
25              var rss:XML = event.result as XML;
26
27              var currTitle:String;
28              var currContent:String;
29
30              var currPost:String;
31              var postList:String;
32
33              //Store all the entry nodes in an xmlList
34              xmlData = rss.entry;
35              postList = "";
36
37              for(var i:int = 0; i<xmlData.length();i++)
38              {
39                  //Extract the current title and content
40                  currTitle = xmlData[i].title;
41                  currContent = xmlData[i].content;
42
43                  //Format the title and content using HTML
44                  currPost = "<p><b>"+currTitle+"</b></p><br>"+"<p>"+currContent+" ... </p><br><br>";
45
46                  //Concatenate the current post to the post list
47                  postList += currPost;
48              }
49
50              //Fetch the post list to the TextArea Component using its htmlText property so the HTML
51              //added to the text is properly interpreted by the textField.
52              display.htmlText = postList;
53          }
54      ]]>
55  </mx:Script>
```

Figure 1-25. The formatting script

21

We also see the creation of a function here called onResult. We will be looking at functions when we explore ActionScript 3.0 in Chapter 7. For now, though, we need to know that a function has to be called in order to work. We call this function in our HTTPService, so that our HTTPService now looks like Figure 1-26.

```
<mx:HTTPService id="feed" url="{urlFeed.text}" resultFormat="e4x" result = "onResult(event);" />
```

Figure 1-26. The changed HTTPService tag

26. Make this change to the HTTPService tag now.

27. Try running the example again. Our RSS output now looks like Figure 1-27.

With that, we have created our first Flex application. With the exception of the code that parsed the XML, this project consisted mostly of pulling together the prebuilt components and connecting them to each other. Hold on to this file—in the next chapter, we will be using Cascading Style Sheets (CSS) to customize the visuals for our Atom Reader.

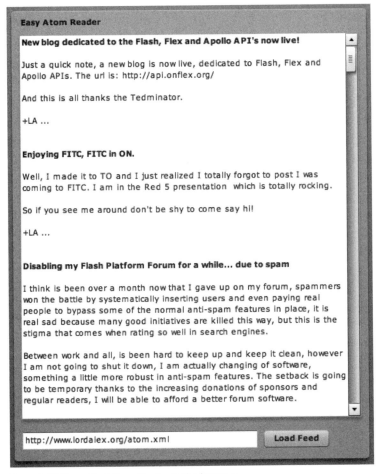

Figure 1-27. Formatted Atom Reader in the browser

22

Summary

With this example, you have started to look at building Flex applications and have become familiar with the Flex Builder interface. You've learned that creating Flex applications revolves around the use of components that are stacked on each other as opposed to being created from scratch. The layout that is created can be seen in the two related views in the MXML Editor, Design and Source. The Source view shows the MXML as code that can be directly modified, while the Design view shows the MXML visually. Any changes that happen in one view affect the other.

You have also seen that working with Flex is done through a relationship between the designer and developer. In the next chapter we'll start to control the look of our applications through CSS styling.

Chapter 2

STYLING

What we'll cover in this chapter:

- Using the Flex Style Explorer
- Modifying component aesthetics through Cascading Style Sheets (CSS)

Files used in this chapter:

- AtomReader-BeforeCSS.zip
- AtomReader-CompleteWithCSS.zip
- CustomStyling1.css

Now that we have built our first application in Chapter 1, we can use it in this chapter to explore changing the visuals. By default, the components have a certain visual look to them, as we saw in Chapter 1. As nice as the folks at Adobe make these default settings, they will always look, well, default. Thankfully, there are some very powerful ways to change the look of a Flex application so that you can create that beautiful, clear interface that you imagine for your applications.

There are three major ways to change the look of a Flex application. The first is called styling, a method that involves setting the style attributes of each component through an external file or styling code. This is a useful approach and one that you will likely use most often. It is efficient, and especially when you use the external file method, fits very well into the workflow.

A second method to change the look of an application is to change its properties. We will be looking at this in Chapter 3, along with how to use states and transitions.

When you want to make a dramatic change to the look of an application, you need to go in and modify the images that create the components. This third method involves changing the SWC files for the components, and Chapters 4 and 5 will show you how to use Fireworks, Illustrator, and Photoshop to do this.

Using styling in Flex

Changing the styling of an application can be tricky at first, but Flex includes a useful tool to make it considerably easier. The Flex Style Explorer is an online tool that can be found at http://examples.adobe.com/flex3/consulting/styleexplorer/Flex3StyleExplorer.html.

The Flex Style Explorer

The Style Explorer (Figure 2-1) lets you interact with components and visually modify them. More importantly, it is an effective development tool that allows you to create CSS within the site and then bring it into your application. In the Style Explorer you can see the effect that changing the styling of a component has and then transfer it over to your project. Let's break this tool down to its separate sections.

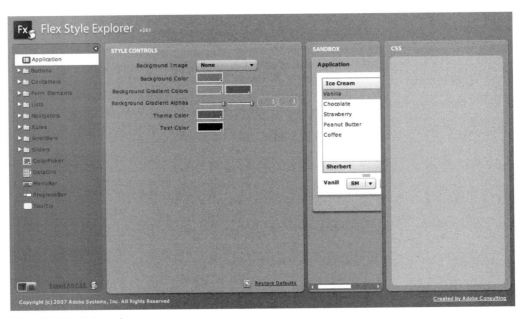

Figure 2-1. Flex Style Explorer

Going left to right, the first section lists all of the components within Flex Builder (Figure 2-2). From this list you select the component that you want to style.

1. Let's start with the Button that we placed in our project to load our feed in Chapter 1 (see Figure 2-3).

Figure 2-2. The list of components in Flex Builder

Figure 2-3. We'll start with the Button component.

Playing with button styles

When you select the Button from the list, you will notice that the section next to the component list changes dramatically (see Figure 2-4). This section shows all the styling attributes that can be changed for a button.

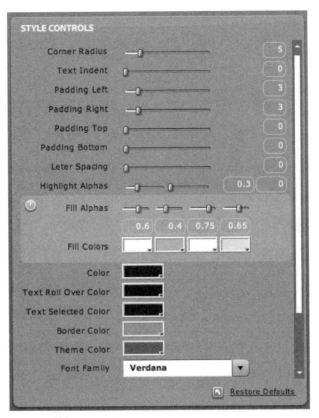

Figure 2-4. Style controls

2. You will notice that there are a large number of attributes that can be changed. Take some time to play around with these attributes.

Don't worry too much about getting your button to look pretty at this point—during your period of experimentation, it's better to make dramatic changes to the attributes to clearly see what they do. You can either change an attribute by moving the slider or by entering a value manually. Any change that you make here will be immediately visible on the example of the component in the section to the right. Many of the attributes are fairly self-explanatory; for example, increasing the value for the corner radius exaggerates the corner rounding on the button. The padding attributes affect the placement of the label. Figure 2-5 shows a button with increased corner rounding, label padding, and letter spacing. Along the bottom of this panel, you'll see a Restore Defaults button. Clicking this button clears any of the changes you have made for this component and lets you try again. Any changes you have made for the other components will not be removed when you click this button.

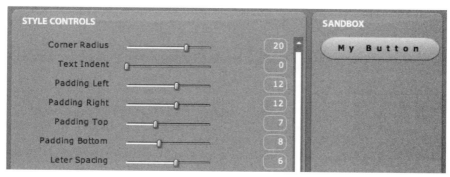

Figure 2-5. Our button with styling

Less immediately understandable are the attributes that dictate the Highlight Alphas and Fill Alphas (Figure 2-6).

It is the Highlight Alphas and the Fill Alphas that give Flex applications their characteristic subtle gradients that add depth. The first Highlight Alphas setting controls the strength of a gradi-

Figure 2-6. Attributes for Highlight Alphas and Fill Alphas

ent that starts from the top, while the second controls the gradient that starts from the midpoint of the button. The first Fill Alphas slider and color selector control the color of the gradient starting from the top, while the second set control the gradient that begins from the bottom of the button while it is in its up state. The third and fourth set control the same visual aspects for the over state. The Theme Color, located further down the list of controls, sets the down state, or highlight, look of the button.

In Figure 2-7 you can see the effects of the changes we've made to our button.

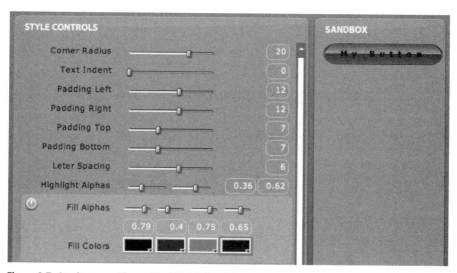

Figure 2-7. Our button with modified Highlight Alphas and Fill Alphas

The rest of the attributes focus mostly on modifying the label on the button (Figure 2-8).

The first three controls allows you to change the text color in its different states. The last three let you change the font and formatting. The ones that are different are the Border Color and Theme Color.

3. The Border Color allows you to change the color of the hairline border along the outside of the button. This is fairly faint, so try a vibrant color to see it well.

Figure 2-8. Button label style controls

A theme within Flex is a set of visual properties, such as highlight or down state color, that define the overall properties. The default theme in Flex is called Halo.

> *The best way to learn how these style attributes affect your components is to play with them for a bit. See how different you can make your buttons!*

CSS in the Style Explorer

The key part of the Style Explorer that makes it a useful tool is the CSS panel.

4. Once you have played around for a bit, have a look at the final section of the Style Explorer, the CSS panel (Figure 2-9).

This final section of the Style Explorer shows us the CSS that creates our changes. All the modifications that we have made to this component are visible here. This is a good time to have a closer look at CSS and the syntax that it uses.

You are probably familiar with working with CSS inside HTML pages. Flex uses a subset of the possible CSS specifications, so not everything that you may have used with HTML will work in Flex. This is partly due to the use of CSS in Flex. In an HTML page, you often use CSS to create the entire layout of the page, separating content from display. With Flex, MXML is used to create the layout. The CSS is mostly used to modify the look, such as color, font, and kerning, instead of affecting the overall layout of the page.

```
CSS
Button {
    cornerRadius: 20;
    paddingLeft: 12;
    paddingRight: 12;
    paddingTop: 7;
    paddingBottom: 7;
    letterSpacing: 6;
    highlightAlphas: 0.36, 0.62;
    fillAlphas: 0.79, 0.4, 0.75, 0.65;
    fillColors: #000066, #ff0000,
#00ccff, #990000;
    color: #333300;
    textRollOverColor: #000099;
    borderColor: #ffffff;
    themeColor: #cc0000;
    fontFamily: Arial;
    fontSize: 16;
    fontWeight: bold;
}
```

Figure 2-9. The CSS panel

Let's have a look at a small piece of the CSS produced in the Style Explorer to help you grasp the syntax. Figure 2-10 shows the CSS for a button with just two properties set.

The CSS is made up of the *selectors*—in this case, Button and a *declaration block*. A declaration block consists of the property and value that you want the component to be set to, enclosed within curly braces. A semicolon is used to separate multiple properties. Most of the possible properties for each component are seen within the Style Explorer, but not all. A complete set of the properties that can be changed with CSS for each component is available in the help files that come with Flex Builder (see Figure 2-11).

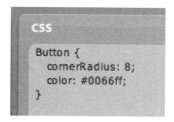

Figure 2-10. The CSS for our button with two properties set

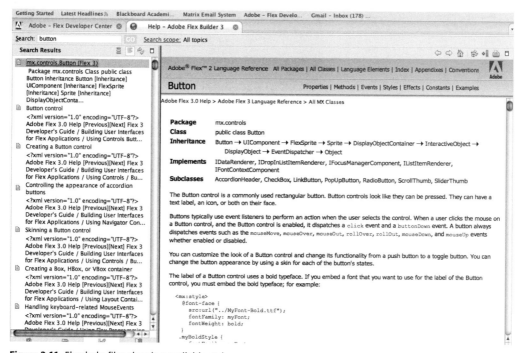

Figure 2-11. Flex help files showing available styles

It is this final section of the Style Explorer that makes it more than just a good learning tool—it is a great development tool as well. All of the changes that we have made through the style controls are converted into CSS code, which is displayed in this area and can be copied into Flex Builder to style the buttons in our project (we'll do this later.) We can copy the CSS directly from here, but let's hold off on that. Instead, let's continue to style the other components that we used in the Atom Reader. The Style Explorer stores all the changes that we make for all the components, and we will be able to copy all the CSS together into Flex Builder.

Styling panels, text areas, and text inputs

As you'll recall, the other major components that we used in the previous chapter were the Panel, TextArea, and TextInput.

5. Let's start with the Panel tab (Figure 2-12)—select it now.

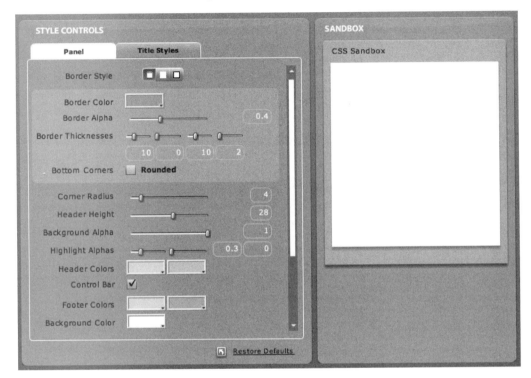

Figure 2-12. The Panel controls

The Panel tab has a few major areas that can be modified. There is the border, the area that surrounds the white content area in the middle. You can set the border style (there are three options), the size, and the color of this area. On top of this color we have the header and footer areas. These use a similar combination of two colors and alpha fades to create a gradient, giving the panel a bit of depth on the top and bottom. The Background Color and Background Alpha define the content area. Figure 2-13 shows an example of a Panel with many of the attributes modified.

You can modify the Title font using the Title Styles tab.

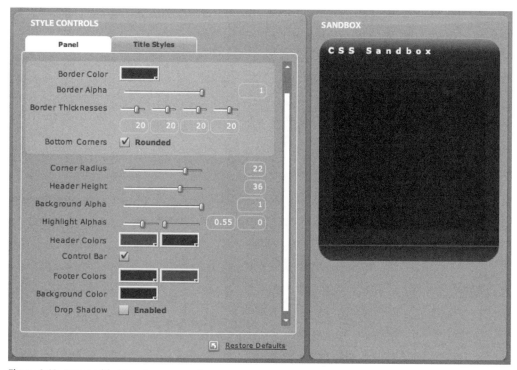

Figure 2-13. Our modifed Panel component

6. Take some time out now to play with the panel styles.

Both the TextArea and TextInput components can be found in the Form Elements folder (Figure 2-14).

Figure 2-14. TextArea component in the Style Explorer

33

The controls for the TextArea and TextInput are nearly identical and allow you to modify many of the attributes that you need to have control over when dealing with text. You can change the padding, indentation, leading, font, and alignment (Figure 2-15).

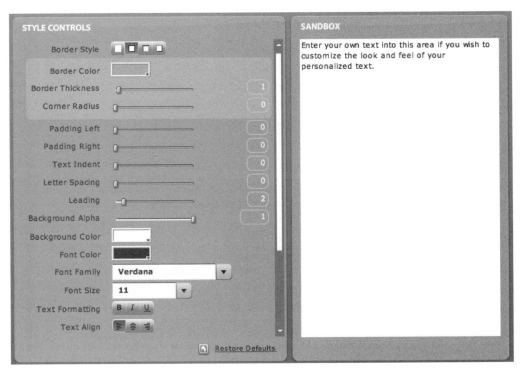

Figure 2-15. TextArea style controls

The settings that are most interesting here are the Border Style settings (see Figure 2-16).

Figure 2-16. TextArea border options

You can see the effects of the changes better if you change the background color first. The first of the options is to have no border at all. This is the simplest of the choices. The second gives you a solid border. This option also allows you to round the corners of your TextArea. The third option is to create an inset border. This option works well to give a little bit of depth to your design and tends to work well with the soft gradients that are often involved with Flex applications. The final option is to create an outset border. Figure 2-17 shows a TextArea with an inset border style.

7. Again, stop and experiment with the settings we've just discussed.

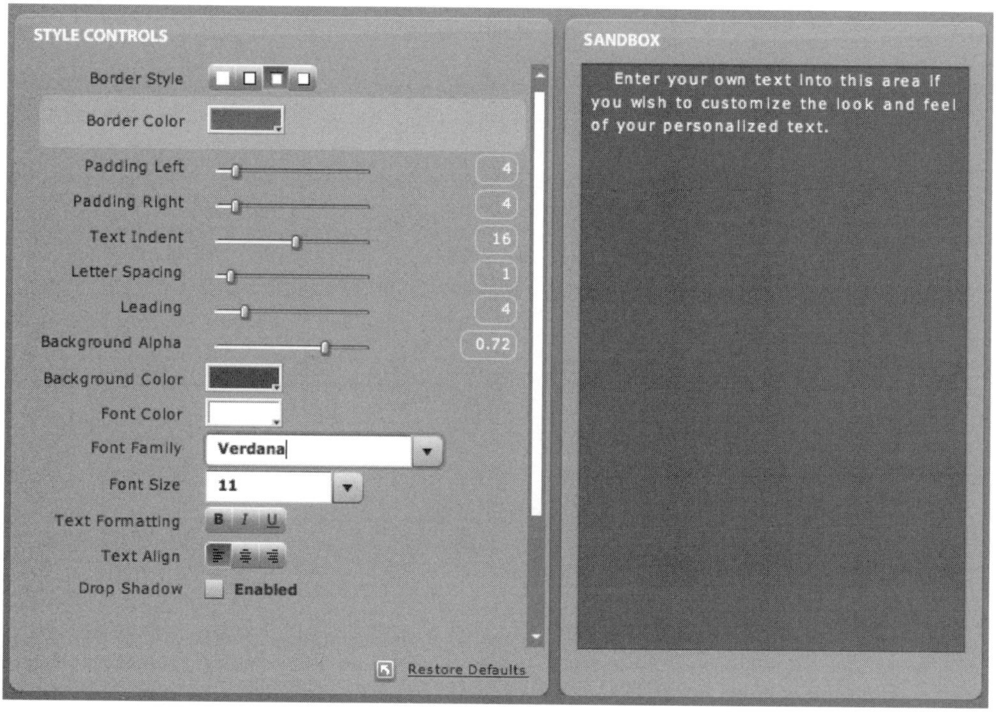

Figure 2-17. Our modified TextArea

Styling the whole application at once

There is still one more part of the project that we want to set the style for before we bring the styling into Flex Builder. Besides being able to style the Flex components, you can also style the application as a whole. This is the first item in the list on the left side (Figure 2-18).

With Application selected, you can modify aspects of your project that cover the whole of the project. One of the useful options is to bring in a background image. Using the Style Explorer, you can change the background from the first pulldown menu (Figure 2-19).

Figure 2-18. Selecting Application from the list

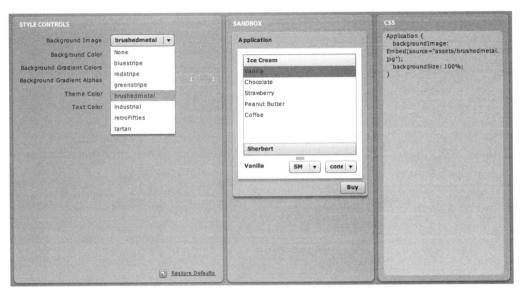

Figure 2-19. Application with a background image added

Now is a good time to have a closer look at the CSS that is created through the style controls.

This example illustrates the consistent structure of the CSS (see Figure 2-20). The important thing to note is the location of the image name. Images that are used in your project should be placed into an "assets" folder. It is good form to create an assets folder to hold these various images and CSS files. We will be coming back to this later in this chapter once we have placed the CSS into our Flex project.

```
CSS

Application {
    backgroundImage:
Embed(source="assets/brushedmetal.
jpg");
    backgroundSize: 100%;
}
```

Figure 2-20. The CSS for the application background image

In the Style Explorer, you can set the background image back to None so that you can see the effects of the other controls. If you mess around with the background color, you'll find that Background Gradient Colors and Background Gradient Alphas tend to create some dramatic effects. We are partial to the effect of orange and gray (Figure 2-21). If you do not want the gradient effect that's there by default, set both Gradient Alphas to 0.

The Theme Color setting allows you to change the dominant color in whichever theme you are using. This is most vividly visible in the selected item color in the example in the Sandbox. The Sandbox is the area in the Style Explorer where the components are shown.

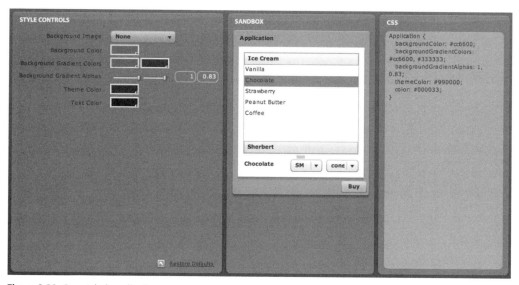

Figure 2-21. Our styled application

8. Our time playing with the Style Explorer is almost over—take a final break to play with some of the Application settings, as we just described, and then move on to the next section.

Getting the style back into our applications

We have now done a good deal of styling in the Style Explorer. The question is how to get that styling to our application. Thankfully the Style Explorer has a great little feature to help us do just this. On the bottom of the first panel, you will find a button named Export All CSS (Figure 2-22). Clicking this button copies all of the CSS that we have built in the Style Explorer into our clipboard.

With the CSS temporarily stored in the clipboard, we can now go back into Flex Builder and bring it in.

1. First create a folder named assets to hold the CSS and any images we may need (Figure 2-23). Make sure that you are in the current project so that the folder is created there.

Figure 2-22. The Export All CSS button

37

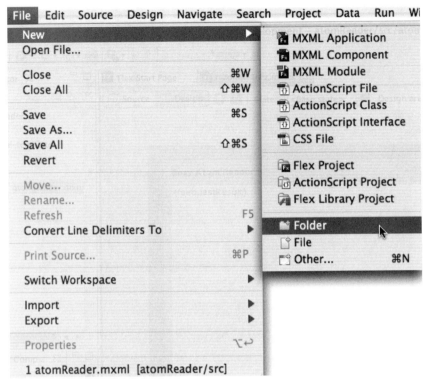

Figure 2-23. Create a new folder.

2. In this same submenu you have the option to create a new CSS file—do so now and call it customStyle1.css.

3. Select the assets folder in the project when the dialog box opens to place the CSS file into that folder. If the file is created elsewhere, you can still drag and drop it into the folder (Figure 2-24).

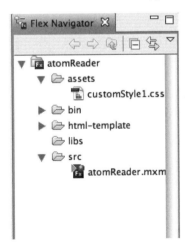

Figure 2-24. Place customStyle1.css in the assets folder.

4. Since the styles that you created have now been copied into the clipboard, you can simply paste (Ctrl+V/Cmd+V) them into the CSS file you created (Figure 2-25)—do so now.

```
Fx Flex Start Page    Fx atomReader.mxml    *customStyle1.css  X

</> Source    Design

 1  Application {
 2      backgroundColor: #cc6600;
 3      backgroundGradientColors: #cc6600, #333333;
 4      backgroundGradientAlphas: 1, 0.83;
 5      themeColor: #990000;
 6      color: #000033;
 7  }
 8
 9  Button {
10      cornerRadius: 20;
11      paddingLeft: 12;
12      paddingRight: 12;
13      paddingTop: 7;|
14      paddingBottom: 7;
15      letterSpacing: 6;
16      highlightAlphas: 0.36, 0.62;
17      fillAlphas: 0.79, 0.4, 0.75, 0.65;
18      fillColors: #000066, #ff0000, #00ccff, #990000;
19      color: #333300;
20      textRollOverColor: #000099;
21      textSelectedColor: #ffffff;
22      borderColor: #ffffff;
23      themeColor: #cc0000;
24      fontFamily: Arial;
25      fontSize: 16;
26      fontWeight: bold;
27  }
28
29  LinkBar {
```

Figure 2-25. Paste the styles pasted into the CSS file.

Now we just have to tell our Flex application to make use of this file. We do this by jumping back into our atomReader.mxml, selecting the source view, and entering an <mx:Style> element to reference our CSS file.

5. Enter the line <mx:Style source="/assets/customStyle1.css"/> just below the opening <mx:Style> tag, as shown in Figure 2-26.

```
Flex Start Page    *atomReader.mxml  X    *customStyle1.css

</> Source    Design

1  <?xml version="1.0" encoding="utf-8"?>
2  <mx:Application xmlns:mx="http://www.adobe.com/2006/mxml" layout="absolute">
3      <mx:Style source="/assets/customStyle1.css"/>
4  <mx:Script>
```

Figure 2-26. This tag connects our Flex application to the CSS file.

6. In order to see the changes to your design, save your file and then run the project again.

The result should be an Atom Reader that looks dramatically different from the original default settings. Your creation will likely look somewhat Frankensteinian at this point as we were focused more on seeing dramatic changes and seeing all of the options for manipulating. Changing all the options on a component is a good way to learn, but not the best way to create a subtle interface. Trying different combinations will make you more familiar with the effects that the CSS has on your design. More subtle use of the styling tends to have a better effect.

A more subtle design

Let's try a new design that uses more subtle changes.

1. To start fresh, first open the Style Explorer in a new browser window.

This time we are going to focus on the Application and Panel components. Selecting colors as you go through the CSS tends to lead to mismatched colors as you do not see all the colors at once. For this reason it is important to set a color scheme at the beginning. Figure 2-27 shows the color scheme that we will be using.

Figure 2-27. Color scheme

2. Give the application background a soft color to avoid distracting from the main content; d8c4a8 works well (Figure 2-28).

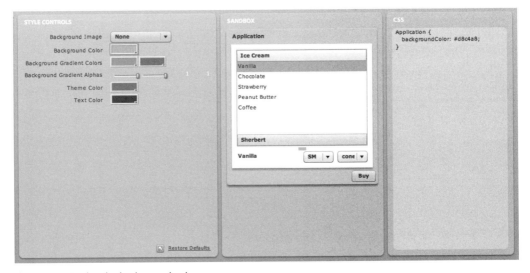

Figure 2-28. Setting the background color

3. In the panel, add some complementary colors to the border, leaving the content area white to get crisp text. You can see the settings we used in Figure 2-29.

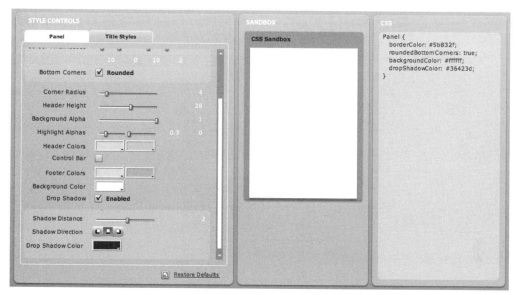

Figure 2-29. Panel styling

For the title, the main concern is to keep the text readable (Figure 2-30).

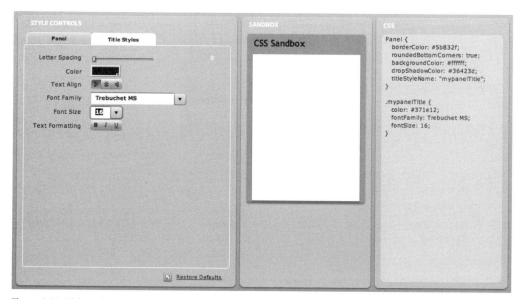

Figure 2-30. Title styling

4. Choose the Title Styles tab in the Style Controls and modify the setting.

5. Now that you've specified all the settings, you can export all the CSS to the clipboard as you did earlier (Figure 2-31).

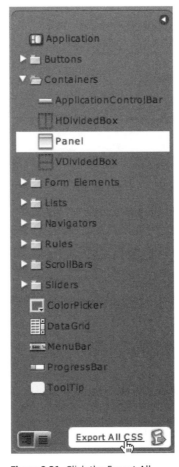

Figure 2-31. Click the Export All CSS button.

6. With the CSS now stored in the clipboard, you can now copy it into your CSS file—copy it into customStyle1.css, replacing what was there before.

7. Run your project again, and it should look like Figure 2-32. The project is now properly styled (well, according to us!).

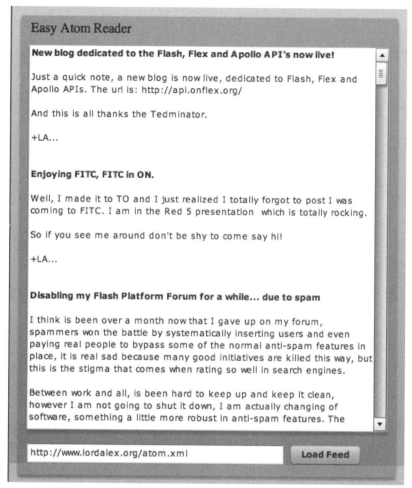

Figure 2-32. Our styled Atom Reader

Summary

In this chapter, you learned how to use CSS to change the look of your applications. The key point is that CSS in Flex is not principally used to control the layout of the design (this is done through MXML). Instead, CSS is a quick and effective way to change the look of your components and application over-all. You can define many features of the components through CSS, including colors, fonts, corner rounding, and alpha gradients. Changing these features using CSS modifies your design so that it does not have a default look.

The Flex Style Explorer is an effective way to alter the CSS for a Flex application, but you can also create the CSS by typing it into a CSS file. Of course, even if you create the CSS through the Style Explorer, you can still modify it by hand if necessary. In the next chapter, we'll look at view states.

Chapter 3

WORKING WITH STATES

What we'll cover in this chapter:

- Creating different view states
- Creating multiple CSS styles for multiple components
- Using absolute layout

Files used in this chapter:

- PersonalPage.zip (completed project)
- style.css
- small1.png
- small2.png
- headshot.png

So far the projects that we have built have been based on having a single page. The Atom Reader brought data in dynamically but showed all of its content at once. With a normal HTML page, showing other information would be done by loading a new page into the browser. In a Flash project, you would show other information by jumping to a different place in the timeline. Since Flex has no timeline (which can get problematic on larger projects) and we want to avoid having page reloads, we bring in new pages by changing the state of the Flex project. View states allow you to create different presentation layouts without having to create separate MXML documents and refresh the browsing window. Changing the states makes some objects disappear and some appear as you need them. In essence, this gives the illusion of multiple pages, but with simpler design and no page reloads.

Building a personal website

Let's illustrate by creating a personal page. The final product will look something like Figure 3-1 and can be found at http://lordalex.org/flex4designers/Chapter%203/bin/PersonalWebsite.html.

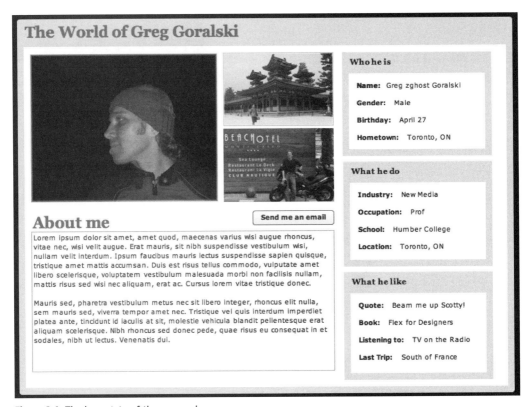

Figure 3-1. The base state of the personal page

This will be the base state of the project, or how it will look on initial load. Clicking the Send me an email button will jump us to our second state, which contains a feedback form that can be used to send Greg an e-mail, as shown in Figure 3-2.

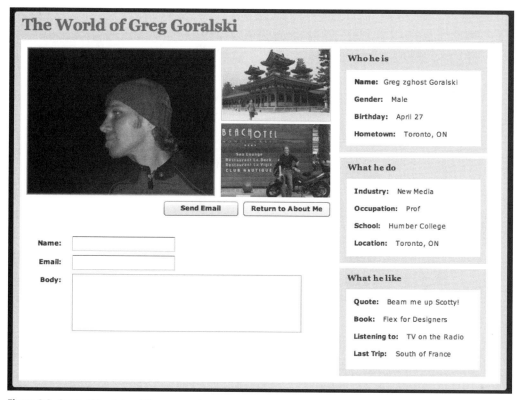

Figure 3-2. ContactMe state of the personal page

This will be called the ContactMe state. As you can see, most of the content is the same and so will not have to be reloaded. Instead, just the bio text becomes hidden and the e-mail form becomes visible. We will not get into making the e-mail form functional, as it is not important for the purpose of this chapter.

Setting up the project

We will be building this project from scratch.

1. Let's get moving on this example by starting a new project (Figure 3-3).

Figure 3-3. Select File ➤ New ➤ Flex Project.

2. Call the project personalPage and place it in the default Flex folder.

Note where the default location of your project is (Figure 3-4). On installation, Flex Builder creates a Flex 3 folder in your documents folder. This serves as the default location for the projects:

- documents/Flex 3/ProjectName (Mac)
- My Documents\Flex 3\ProjectName (Windows)

We will be adding files to this folder later in this chapter.

Figure 3-4. Creating personalPage

We also need to set up a folder for our assets, namely our CSS and images.

3. Select File ➤ New ➤ Folder, and name the new folder assets.

Building the base state

As with many new projects, we need to first start with a Panel component. It is here that we will be placing all our other components. The Panel component also provides a title for our page and keeps the entire project centered in the browser. When you first place a component on the page, feel free to place it in the general area of where you want it to be. We will be using an absolute layout for this project, so it will be easiest to modify the layout through the properties of the individual components (Figure 3-5).

4. Place a Panel component in the Design view.

Let's set the properties for this main panel. The title will be the main title on the page. We will use The World of Greg Goralski, but you can put in your own name. Really, we don't mind.

In the layout properties, we set the overall size and the constraints. You can tinker with the height and width as you build your project; ours ended up being 730 pixels wide and 550 pixels tall so these are the numbers we'll use. We want the design to be centered with a bit of space along the top, so we specify this using the layout handles. Set either of the left or right layout handles to center. This will keep our panel centered within the browser. Set the top layout handle to anchor with an offset of 10. Our final Layout panel looks like Figure 3-6.

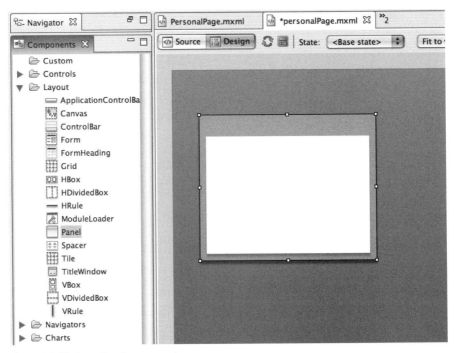

Figure 3-5. Placing a Panel component

5. Set the properties for the panel.

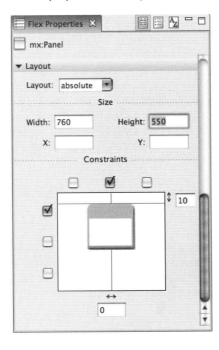

Figure 3-6. Layout for the main panel

Next, bring in the images that are to take up the first area. In our design we have three images: a larger headshot image, called headshot.png, and two smaller images next to it, called small1.png and small2.png. If you want to bring your own images in, it is important to set their size in a program like Photoshop first. This keeps the images looking crisper and with a smaller file size than if you bring them into Flex Builder and have them scaled there. It is generally best to modify and refine any images inside Photoshop before bringing them into Flex as Photoshop is very effective at image manipulation. We will be seeing more of this in Chapter 5. The headshot image is 295 pixels by 224 pixels, and the smaller images are 170 pixels by 110 pixels each. While these images are in Photoshop, it is a good time to add a border if you like. By adding a border in Photoshop, using the Pen tool or any other method you want, the border will become a part of the image. This means that no extra processing power is needed to display the border.

6. Copy the images into your assets folder for this project. To find the assets folder, go to the folder that was created for the project (Figure 3-4).

You can find the image component in the Controls folder in the Components panel (Figure 3-7).

7. Drag an image component onto the panel you created.

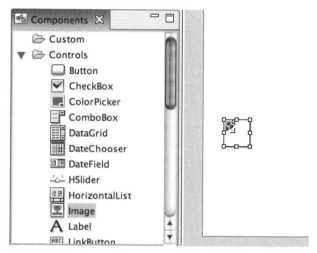

Figure 3-7. Dragging an image component

8. Enter the file name of the image in the Source field in Properties to bring it in and set the size of the component to match the image (Figure 3-8).

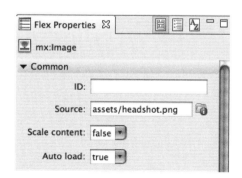

Figure 3-8. Specifying the image name

51

For the layout, you can drag and drop it into the place that you want it. Guidelines will appear to help you align the image with other components. If you want to do more detailed movements, use the arrow keys to move the component one pixel in any direction. If you hold down Shift as you press the arrow keys, the component will move 5 pixels at a time.

9. Place the image where you want it to end up in the final design (Figure 3-9).

Figure 3-9. Positioning the image

10. Repeat the same process to bring in the other two images—try to end up with something like Figure 3-10.

Figure 3-10. All images in position

11. Next bring in the panels along the right side of the page.

Each of these panels is the same component as the main panel. Bring one in and set its title to be Who he is (or Who she is, as the case may be). This will be the profile area. Do not worry about the size of the panel just yet—it will be dependent on the amount of content you want to put in (Figure 3-11).

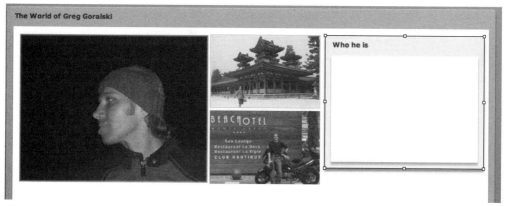

Figure 3-11. Our personal page design with the "Who he is" panel added

The easiest way to bring the text into the panel is through a series of labels. The Label component can be found in the Controls folder and is essentially a simple piece of text that you can put just about anywhere.

12. Build the content of the panel by placing a label for each topic.

The automatic guidelines are very useful when doing a layout like this (Figure 3-12).

The topic titles, such as Name:, should be bolded, while the remaining text should have no bolding. Once you have filled in all the text, you can change the size of the panel, as shown in Figure 3-13.

Figure 3-12. Automatic guidelines

Figure 3-13. Resizing the panel

13. Repeat the same process to create the other two panels on the right side (Figure 3-14).

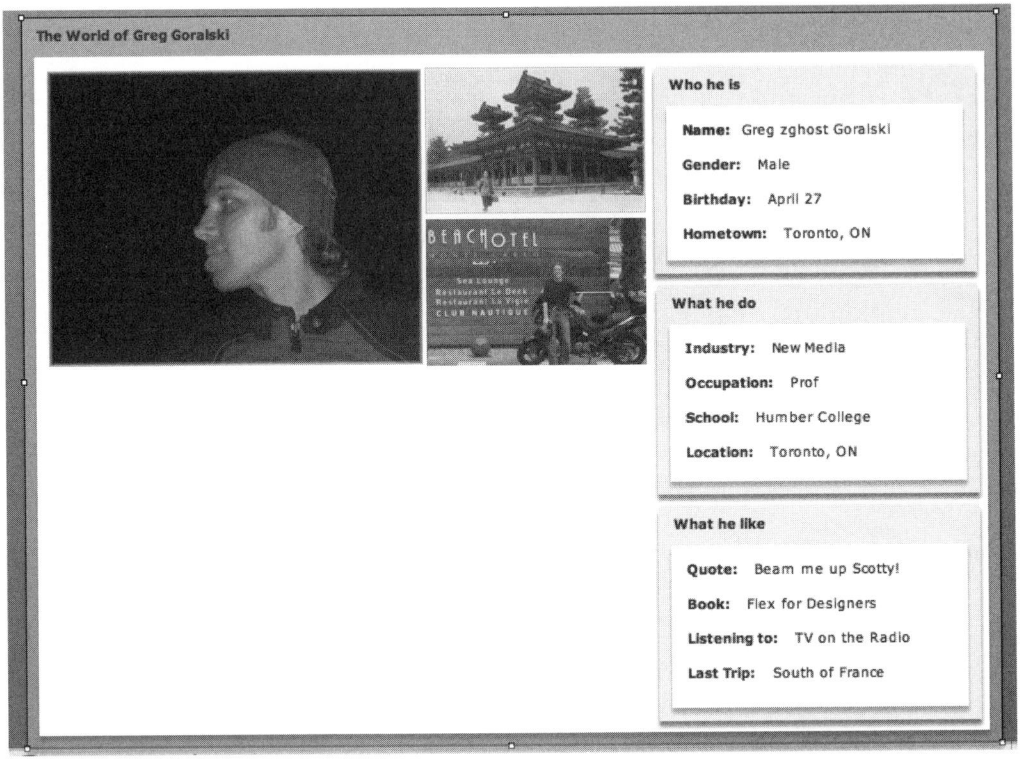

Figure 3-14. The personal page with images and panels

The text below the images will change when the Send me an email button is clicked, but we'll build it using the same techniques.

14. Bring in a TextArea component and fill it with either your bio or greeked text.

You can double-click on a TextArea component to enter text. At this point, also add a label and a button above the text area, as shown in Figure 3-15.

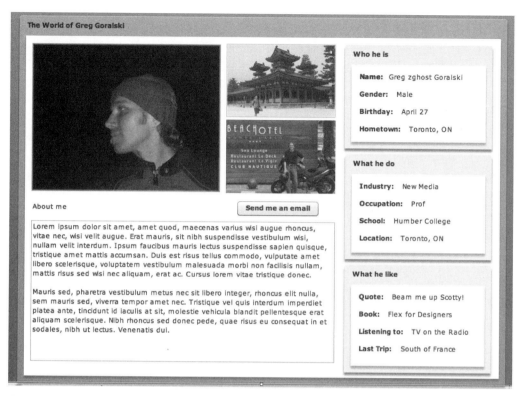

The World of Greg Goralski

Who he is

Name: Greg zghost Goralski

Gender: Male

Birthday: April 27

Hometown: Toronto, ON

What he do

Industry: New Media

Occupation: Prof

School: Humber College

Location: Toronto, ON

About me

Send me an email

Lorem ipsum dolor sit amet, amet quod, maecenas varius wisi augue rhoncus, vitae nec, wisi velit augue. Erat mauris, sit nibh suspendisse vestibulum wisi, nullam velit interdum. Ipsum faucibus mauris lectus suspendisse sapien quisque, tristique amet mattis accumsan. Duis est risus tellus commodo, vulputate amet libero scelerisque, voluptatem vestibulum malesuada morbi non facilisis nullam, mattis risus sed wisi nec aliquam, erat ac. Cursus lorem vitae tristique donec.

Mauris sed, pharetra vestibulum metus nec sit libero integer, rhoncus elit nulla, sem mauris sed, viverra tempor amet nec. Tristique vel quis interdum imperdiet platea ante, tincidunt id iaculis at sit, molestie vehicula blandit pellentesque erat aliquam scelerisque. Nibh rhoncus sed donec pede, quae risus eu consequat in et sodales, nibh ut lectus. Venenatis dui.

What he like

Quote: Beam me up Scotty!

Book: Flex for Designers

Listening to: TV on the Radio

Last Trip: South of France

Figure 3-15. The personal page base state layout with content

The button should have the label *Send me an email*; it will be used to jump to the next state. The label on the left should have the text *About me* and is there to make the layout look pretty.

15. Create the button and label.

We have now built the layout for the project the way we want it to be when the project first opens. This is known as the base state. We now want to create a new state to show what we want to make the layout look like in the next page.

Creating a new state

In the Design view, the States panel should by default be open above the component's Properties. If this is not visible on your screen, you can open the States panel by selecting Window ➤ States, as shown in Figure 3-16.

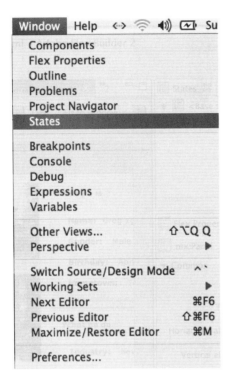

Figure 3-16. Seleting the States option to make the States panel appear

16. Here, create a new state for our project (Figure 3-17).

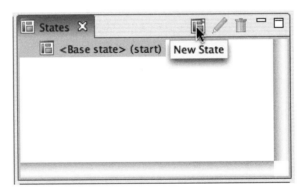

Figure 3-17. The States panel, with the New State button highlighted

17. Name the state and assign the state you want it to be based on.

In this case, it is easy since we only have one previous state, the base state (Figure 3-18).

At first, very little will appear to have changed. Our layout still looks identical. This is because this new state is based off our previous state. But the changes that we perform on this new state will not affect the original base state.

Figure 3-18. Creating a new state

When you want to make changes to a new state, just make sure that the new state is selected in the States *panel and that you are not making unwanted changes to your original states!*

18. For this new state, remove the TextArea, the Send me an email button, and the About me label to make room for the layout of an e-mail form (Figure 3-19).

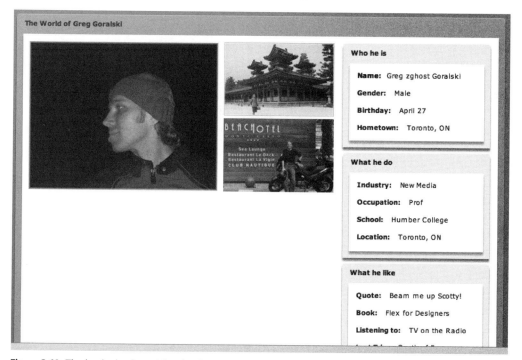

Figure 3-19. The beginning layout for the ContactMe state

To create the new layout, let's use the Form component. The Form component allows you to place all the pieces of your form, in this case, TextAreas and TextInputs, onto one component and move them around together. The Form component also does one more very neat thing: it adds a label next to the component that you place on top of it. This saves time and keeps things aligned.

19. Drag a Form component onto the project and stretch it out to cover the area that you want in your layout. Onto this component, add a TextInput (Figure 3-20).

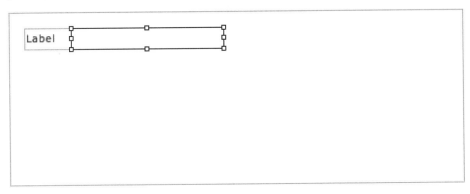

Figure 3-20. Our form with a TextInput component

Notice that the TextInput automatically becomes aligned and gets a label next to it. The Form component is meant for structured forms, and so follows tighter alignment rules.

20. Change the name of the label, either by double-clicking it or by changing the properties, to Name:.

21. Bring in a second TextInput for the sender's e-mail address, and a TextArea for the body of the e-mail (Figure 3-21).

22. Add two buttons to this form, one a Send button that would normally send the e-mail that is written, and a back button to let the user get back to the first state.

This second button will be labeled Return to About Me. Now the form is complete. Make sure you place the Send Email and Return to About Me buttons outside the form area or these buttons will get labels and be aligned with the form elements—that is not what we want. Your form should now look like Figure 3-22.

We will be using the two buttons that we have created, the Send Email button in the base state and the Return to About Me button in the ContactMe state to jump between states.

Figure 3-22. Our complete form

23. Click the base state in the States panel to jump back to the base state (Figure 3-23).

Figure 3-23. States panel showing the base and ContactMe states

If all things work out well, you should see the bio text area that we created earlier.

24. Select the Send Email button. In the properties, to control what we want to happen when the button is clicked, we place the action in the On click property field. In this case, we want to change the current state. Type currentState='contactMe' in this field (Figure 3-24).

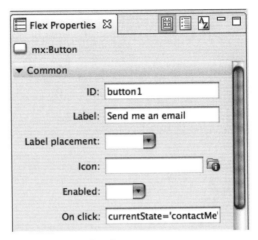

Figure 3-24. Changing the state

25. Jumping back to the ContactMe state, you can do the same for the Return to About Me button. This time, since we have not given the base state a name, we can leave the name area blank. It will look like Figure 3-25.

Figure 3-25. Properties for the button that switches to back state

Styling the project

Now it's time to turn our attention to styling the project. The most commonly used component in this Flex application is the Panel, so we will be focusing our styling on this component. The other components will be largely unstyled.

In this project we have used the Panel component multiple times and in different ways. It is used as a large component that holds the entire project and also as a series of smaller components that hold our text. We may want to have different styling for each of these two cases, but if we use the technique that we used in Chapter 2, where we exported all the CSS at once, all Panel components will get the same styling.

The trick is to pull out the CSS styling piece by piece instead of all at once.

26. Start by creating a new CSS file called style inside the project as shown in Figure 3-26.

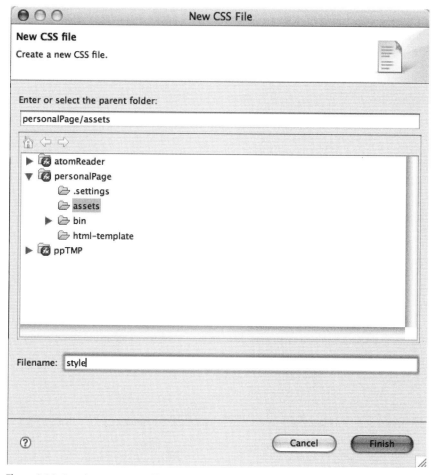

Figure 3-26. Creating a new CSS file

We will still use Flex Style Explorer to get the bulk of the CSS, but we'll modify some of it to make our panels have different styles.

27. Open the Flex Style Explorer and select the Panel component (Figure 3-27).

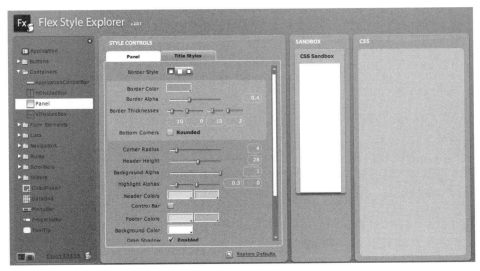

Figure 3-27. Using the Style Explorer to create styling CSS for our panel

28. For the Panel component, set the border color to a lighter color, for example, #fce6b9. Notice that as soon as you do that, the color of the border changes and the CSS for that change appears in the CSS panel in the Style Explorer (Figure 3-28).

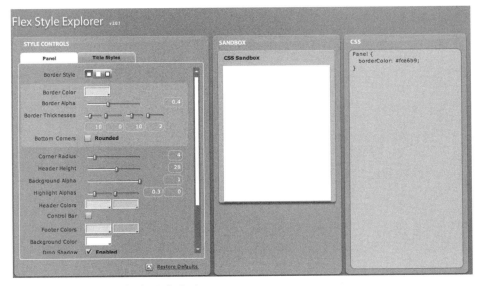

Figure 3-28. Color change in the Style Explorer

29. Copy and paste this CSS straight from here into the CSS file in the Flex project (Figure 3-29).

```
1
2  /* CSS file */
3  Panel {
4      borderColor: #fce6b9;
5  }
6
```

Figure 3-29. Paste the CSS from the panel into the CSS file in the Flex project.

30. Continue to make the changes with the Style Explorer that you want to see on the main Panel component (Figure 3-30). Then copy and paste the CSS that is generated into your CSS file.

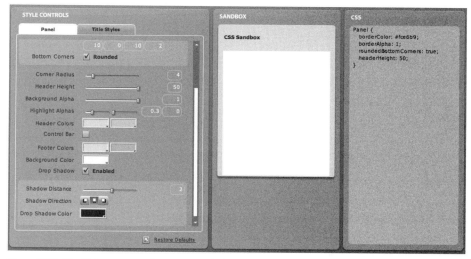

Figure 3-30. Modifying our panel component in the Style Explorer

You should end up with a CSS file that looks like Figure 3-31.

```
1
2  /* CSS file */
3  Panel {
4      borderColor: #fce6b9;
5  }
6  Panel {
7      borderColor: #fce6b9;
8      borderAlpha: 1;
9      roundedBottomCorners: true;
10     headerHeight: 50;
11 }
```

Figure 3-31. Pasting the styling CSS from the Style Explorer into our CSS file in Flex Builder

We want to make this CSS file have multiple styles for different panels. We do this by creating substyles, which involves changing the second panel's CSS to start with a dot and the name for the style—in this case, .mainPanel. We can also remove the second border color to avoid repetition so that we end up with the CSS in Figure 3-32.

```
1
2   /* CSS file */
3   Panel {
4       borderColor: #fce6b9;
5   }
6   .mainPanel {
7       borderAlpha: 1;
8       roundedBottomCorners: true;
9       headerHeight: 50;
10  }
```

Figure 3-32. Our styling CSS with style and substyles

Have a look at what happens when you modify the title styles for the panel (in the Title Styles tab), as shown in Figure 3-33.

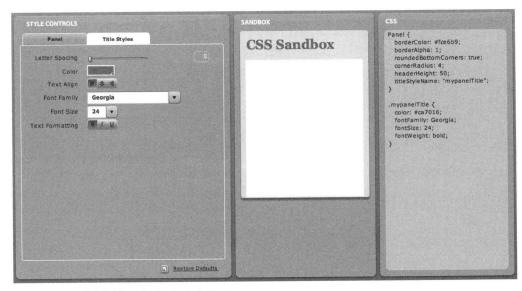

Figure 3-33. Modified title styles in the Style Explorer

Modifying the title styles provides the CSS for the title as a separate piece of CSS under the heading .mypanelTitle that will need to be connected to the panel you want to associate it with. We need to copy this CSS into our CSS file and then modify it. We also have to change the name so that it shows which panel it is associated with; in this case, we can use .mainPanelTitle. We then have to be explicit that this connects with our mainPanel. The code for this step looks like this:

```
titleStyleName: "mainPanelTitle";
```

and should be placed in the .mainPanel CSS.

31. Change your CSS file so that it looks like Figure 3-34.

```
 1
 2  /* CSS file */
 3  Panel {
 4      borderColor: #fce6b9;
 5  }
 6  .mainPanel{
 7      borderAlpha: 1;
 8      roundedBottomCorners: true;
 9      headerHeight: 50;
10      titleStyleName: "mainPanelTitle";
11  }
12
13  .mainPanelTitle {
14      fontFamily: Georgia;
15      color: #ca7016;
16      fontSize: 24;
17      fontWeight: bold;
18  }
```

Figure 3-34. The styling CSS for our panel with substyles in Flex Builder

Let's continue to do the same for the right-side panels. Your CSS file should end up as shown in Figure 3-35.

32. While we are here, let's also set the backgroundColor to black.

Just as we did in Chapter 2, we now need to enter the code into the MXML file that calls on the CSS file.

```
 1  Application {
 2      backgroundColor: #000000;
 3  }
 4
 5  Panel {
 6      borderColor:#fce6b9;
 7      borderAlpha: 1;
 8  }
 9
10  .mainPanel{
11      borderAlpha: 1;
12      roundedBottomCorners: true;
13      headerHeight: 40;
14      titleStyleName: "mainPanelTitle";
15  }
16
17  .mainPanelTitle {
18      fontFamily: Georgia;
19      color: #ca7016;
20      fontSize: 24;
21      fontWeight: bold;
22  }
23
24  .rightPanel{
25      cornerRadius: 0;
26      dropShadowEnabled: false;
27      headerHeight: 30;
28      titleStyleName: "rightPanelTitle";
29  }
30
31  .rightPanelTitle {
32      fontFamily: Georgia;
33      fontSize: 12;
34      color: #333333;
35      fontWeight: bold;
36  }
```

Figure 3-35. Our final CSS file

33. In the Source view of our project, add the code in Figure 3-36.

```
Source    Design
1  <?xml version="1.0" encoding="utf-8"?>
2  <mx:Application xmlns:mx="http://www.adobe.co
3  <mx:Style source="/assets/style.css"/>
4
```

Figure 3-36. This code associates the MXML with the CSS.

Let's jump back to the Design view so that we can tell Flex which panel we want to associate with each piece of CSS. In the Design view if you look at the properties of the panel, you will see that the Style pulldown menu contains the names that we gave to our CSS (Figure 3-37).

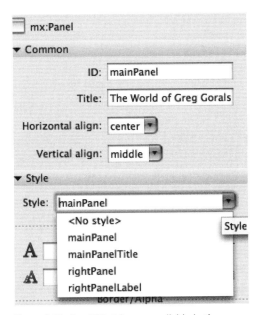

Figure 3-37. Our CSS styles are available in the pulldown menu.

34. Select the correct CSS style for each of the panels and you will find that you can set different styles for different panels.

Figure 3-38 shows one of the panels with the rightPanel style applied and the second without it. You can see that the color is the same on both—we set the color in the Universal panel style we created. However, the other aspects of the panel (namely, the sharp corners, font, and lack of drop shadow) are specified by the rightPanel CSS.

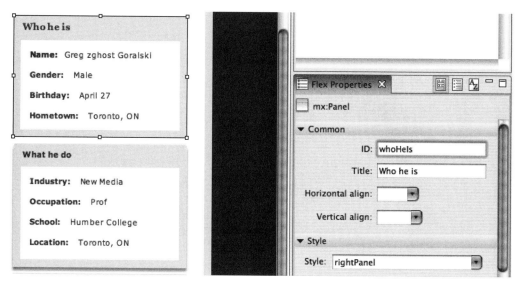

Figure 3-38. Panels with two different styles

The same process applies if you want to have different styles for your other components. The label About Me changed through its properties to fit in with the CSS styling.

35. Change the properties of the About Me label to match Figure 3-39.

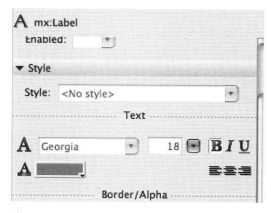

Figure 3-39. About Me label properties

36. With this complete, run your project and see how the different styling affects each set of Panel components—the project should look like Figure 3-40.

Figure 3-40. Our styled personal page

Summary

In this chapter, we explored how to use states to show different information. States are useful because they let you create the illusion of multiple pages without the need for a page refresh. Numerous states can be created in one page by defining a state and changing the components that are presented in that state. Moving between states is done through an event of some sort, often a button click.

We also looked at how to style different instances of a component in different ways using CSS. This allows you to set a different look for a component, for example a Panel, depending on where it is being used. Associating different CSS tags with different instances of a component is done by creating a substyle. You then connect the substyle to a particular instance of a component through the style property.

In the next chapter we will start looking at how Flex interacts with other programs. Specifically we use Fireworks to create a Flex layout.

Chapter 4

FLEX AND FIREWORKS

What we'll cover in this chapter:

- Scaling components in Fireworks
- Matching size or images and components
- Alignment
- Exporting layouts to Flex Builder

Files used in this chapter:

- background.jpg
- fish.png
- KyotoTemple.jpg
- wedding.jpg

We mentioned in the first chapter that Flex plays well with graphics programs—in the case of Fireworks CS3, it is more like they are so close, they finish each other's sentences. Fireworks CS3 comes with some specifically built tools that allow you to create the layouts for your Flex project in Fireworks and then export them into Flex Builder. This enables you to leverage the graphics tools of Fireworks and lets you design within an environment that you may already be familiar with.

Along with the new features of Fireworks, such as new symbols and Scale 9, there is an export feature that lets you save a layout in Fireworks complete with the MXML that can build it in Fireworks.

Creating a Flex layout in Fireworks

In this chapter, we'll start by building a layout in Fireworks that combines images and Flex components. We'll then export that layout as an MXML file that we'll bring into Flex Builder.

1. Begin by opening Fireworks and creating a new document, as shown in Figure 4-1.

Even though you'll later export this document to Flex Builder, you don't need to do anything special at this point—create the document as you would any other design in Fireworks.

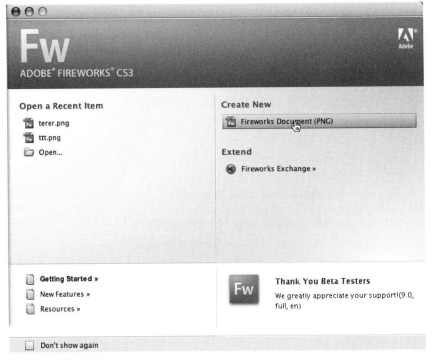

Figure 4-1. Click the Fireworks Document (PNG) button.

It is important to set the size for your project properly at this stage as the layout that Fireworks creates is an *absolute* layout—which means that the position of each element is fixed. This also means that the overall size of the project, once it is imported into Flex Builder, will be the size of the Fireworks document that you set when you first defined the project.

2. Set the size to 800 by 600, the canvas color to white, and the resolution to 72, as shown in Figure 4-2.

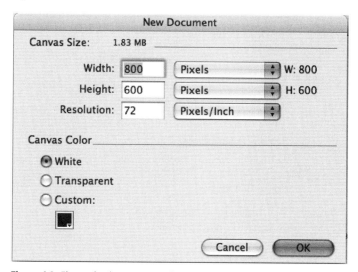

Figure 4-2. Fireworks document settings

A size of 800 by 600 pixels is a standard starting point. It provides a fair amount of room for your elements while still fitting on the lower display resolutions of laptops. It is often easy to forget that not everyone will see your work on a screen resolution as large as the one in your studio.

Importing and manipulating images in Fireworks

In this chapter, you'll be creating a layout for a project that has content similar to the personal page you created in Chapter 3. That is, it will have three small images, three panels with text, and a larger text area. But let's start by adding a new feature: a background image. The key to selecting a background image is to get an image that provides space for the content elements. This often comes in the form of an area that has a consistent color. The image that we've selected for this project is of a temple in Japan—the image fades out to white along the right side. Our plan is to have it fade into the white background color and give us space for our content.

3. Import the image called background.jpg into Fireworks using the File ➤ Import command, as shown in Figure 4-3.

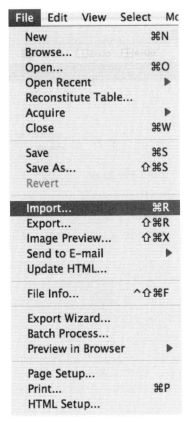

Figure 4-3. Choose Import from the File menu.

Fireworks does not bring the image in with its original size; instead, it has you draw a rectangle for the image in the stage while maintaining its aspect ratio. You want to bring the image in so that it fills most of the height of your page but still provides you with a good deal of white along the right side. You will need to stretch the image using the Scale tool (shown selected in Figure 4-4) to get the right look, as shown in Figure 4-5. This will distort your image somewhat, so be careful not to do this too much. To prevent distortion, you can hold down the Shift key as you use the Scale tool. This will change the size but maintain the aspect ratio of the image.

Figure 4-4. Select the Scale tool.

4. Position and scale the image as shown in Figure 4-5.

Figure 4-5. Imported background image

Organizing Flex Components in Fireworks

One of the reasons that Fireworks plays so well with Flex is that Fireworks has a library of Flex components. This means that you can, while staying in Fireworks, place Flex components such as combo boxes and panels onto your layout. The layout that you create in Fireworks then already has the components in place—without you having to use code—when it is imported into Flex Builder. Our next step is to bring in the Flex components, which you'll find in the Common Library.

5. In Fireworks, open the Common Library by selecting Window ➤ Common Library (see Figure 4-6) or by pressing F7.

The Common Library (shown in Figure 4-7) contains a variety of elements, such as bullets, that are used repeatedly in designs, but most importantly for us, it contains the most commonly used Flex components.

6. Drag a Panel component onto the canvas and copy it two times.

Copying the one panel two times is an easier way to get three identical copies. When you drag in a second Panel component from the Common Library, you'll see a dialog box asking if you want to replace the item that is already in the document. Since we are not modifying the components in Fireworks, we don't need to worry about this. You copy a component in Fireworks in the same way you do in other software applications. With the component selected, you can use the top menu bar and select Edit ➤ Copy followed by Edit ➤ Paste. You can also use the shortcut keys Ctrl+C/Cmd+C and Ctrl+V/Cmd+V.

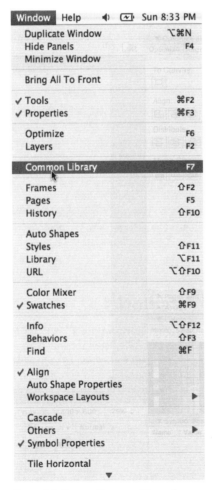

Figure 4-6. Choose Common Library from the Window menu.

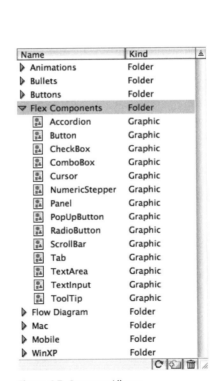

Figure 4-7. Common Library

7. Place the copies roughly in the same locations as shown in Figure 4-8, although the exact position isn't critical for now. We'll align the panels later with the other pieces of our layout.

Figure 4-8. Panel components in place

Our design will have a large text area designed to hold the bulk of our content. Let's now add a TextArea component that will hold the main text. When you first place a TextArea component, it will be rather small.

8. Use the Scale tool to make the component about the size you want it in the final layout, as shown in Figure 4-9.

The text area should be about the same height and twice the width of the Panel components you placed earlier.

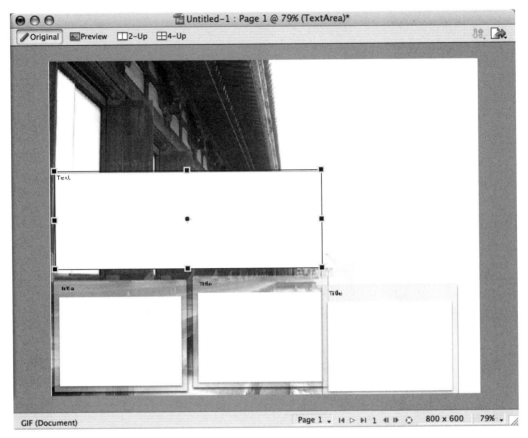

Figure 4-9. TextArea component in place

Our layout is now beginning to overcrowd our background image. We can put a slight transparency on our TextArea to let the background show through. You specify this using the Properties panel that is generally located along the bottom of the window. A transparency of 80% works well; below that, and the text becomes more difficult to read.

   9. Set the transparency of the TextArea to 80 by selecting the TextArea and adjusting the transparency slider in the properties, as shown in Figure 4-10.

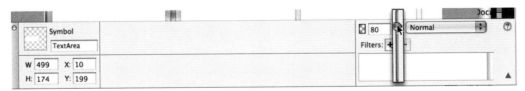

Figure 4-10. TextArea component properties

The file created by Fireworks will "remember" this change in the transparency and add it as a property of the component when we bring it into Flex Builder.

Bring in the three small images that you want to use or use the three provided in the code download for this book at www.friendsofed.com. The three images provided are named fish.png, temple.jpg, and wedding.jpg.

10. Bring the three images in with the rough position and size that you want them to ultimately be. Your layout should look like Figure 4-11.

Don't worry about the file size of the original images. When you export the layout, the images will be compressed so that they are appropriate for web use.

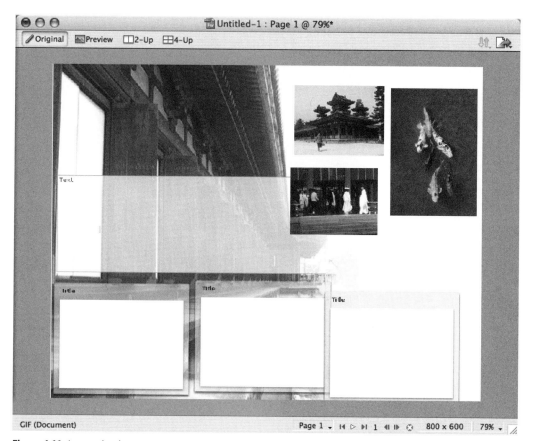

Figure 4-11. Images in place

You also want to place a title in the open space above the TextArea. Normally in Flex Builder you'd create this using a label, but since a label is not one of the available components in Fireworks, you'll use the Text tool (shown selected in Figure 4-12). This gives you more control over the typography than is normally available inside Flex Builder.

11. Use the Text tool in Fireworks to create a title of Fireworks Layout in the space above the TextArea component (top left).

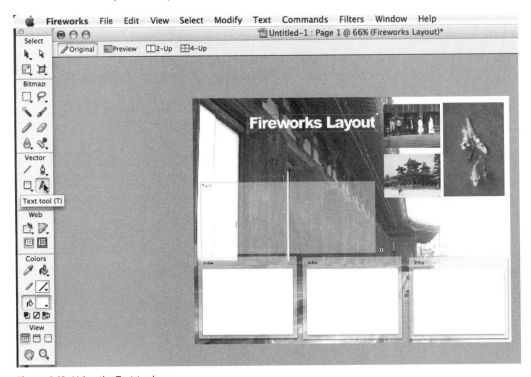

Figure 4-12. Using the Text tool

Using Fireworks to align and refine a layout

Now that we have all the components on our page, we can start working on what Fireworks is really good at in this process: aligning and layout.

12. Open the Align panel, if it is not already open, by selecting Window ➤ Align, as shown in Figure 4-13.

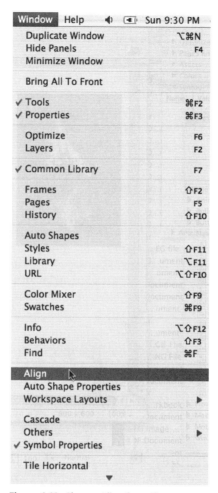

Figure 4-13. Choose Align from the Window menu.

The Align panel gives you a variety of ways to modify the position and scale of the components, as shown in Figure 4-14.

Let's start with organizing our images.

13. Select the images of the temple and wedding. Select Match width and height in the Align tool.

Figure 4-15 shows the images as slightly different sizes. Once you select Match width and height, both images will have the same size, helping you to create a tight, clean layout.

14. Align the two images along their left edge (see Figure 4-16).

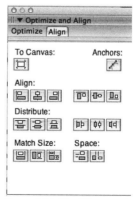

Figure 4-14. The Align panel

81

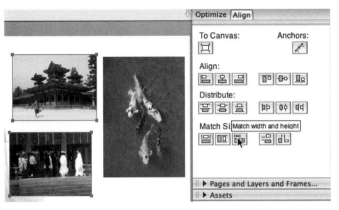

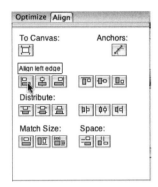

Figure 4-15. Select Match width and height.

Figure 4-16. Select Align left edge.

You can bring the images closer together or further apart one pixel at a time by using the arrow keys. Holding down Shift will move them 5 pixels at a time. The third image poses a slightly tougher challenge. You want to make it the same height as the temple and wedding images combined, but if you stretch it out while maintaining the aspect ratio it becomes too wide, making the layout look unbalanced. Instead, you can crop it to a more appropriate shape. To begin, select Edit ➤ Crop Selected Bitmap (see Figure 4-17) and then adjust the size of the selected area (see Figure 4-18).

Figure 4-17. Select Crop Selected Bitmap from the Edit menu.

Figure 4-18. Adjust the size of the selected area.

15. Crop the fish image.

You can now use the same scale and align tools (as shown in Figure 4-15) to adjust the size of the image so that it creates a tight set of images (see Figure 4-19).

16. Align all three images.

Figure 4-19. Our finished images

Once you have your images set up as you want in relation to one another, it is a good idea to group them.

17. Group the images by pressing Ctrl+G/Cmd+G.

Modifying the images

Grouping the items will allow you to move them around without messing up their alignment to one another. This is also a good time to do any image modifications. Since Fireworks is first and foremost a graphics program, you can make a variety of changes to your images (such as changing color saturation or adding filters) that you can't do in Flex Builder. For this example, you'll add a border by drawing a rectangle with no fill around the images and then add an effect. Fireworks has access to Photoshop Live Effects, a variety of nondestructive effects that you can apply to your images. As Figure 4-20 shows, you can access these effects via the Properties panel.

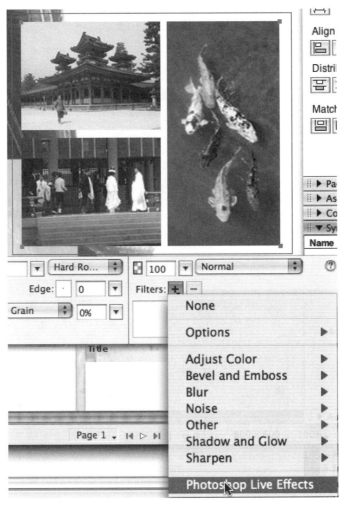

Figure 4-20. Choose Photoshop Live Effects.

You can layer a variety of Photoshop Live Effects on top of each other, but for this example let's just add an inside shadow.

18. Add an inner shadow effect to your images, as shown in Figure 4-21.

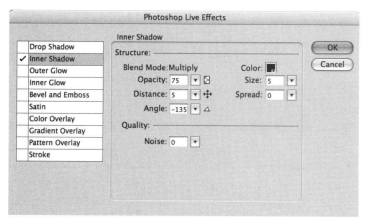

Figure 4-21. Choose Inner Shadow in Photoshop Live Effects.

19. Adjust the scale and alignment of your elements until they are in the final location that you want for the layout (see Figure 4-22).

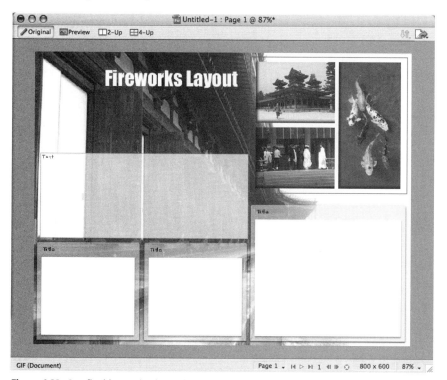

Figure 4-22. Our final layout in Fireworks

Bringing the layout into Flex Builder

To bring the layout into Flex Builder, you need to create a project for it. Without shutting down Fireworks, you'll open Flex Builder and create a new Flex project.

20. Create a new project in Flex Builder named Chapter4 (see Figure 4-23).

Note the location where the project will be created. This is the location where you'll need to save the Fireworks layout.

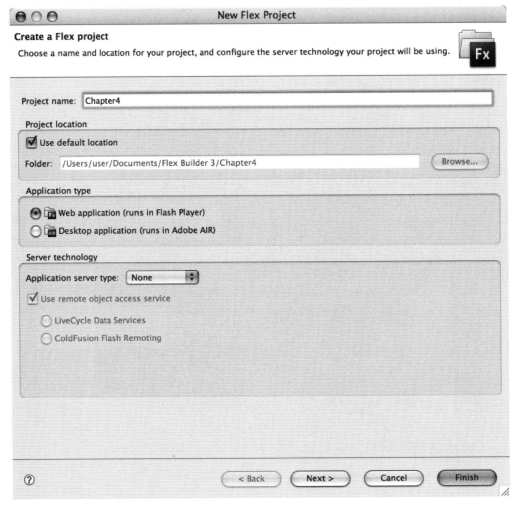

Figure 4-23. Creating a new project in Flex

21. Jumping back to Fireworks, export the document by choosing File ➤ Export.

Fireworks exports to a variety of formats. The interesting thing is that it can export the images along with the MXML for all components. You can then place these files in the Chapter4 folder that Flex

Builder created for the new Flex project. You can also place the images that you used into their own images folder to keep the file structure neat.

22. In Fireworks, name the file fireworksLayout and save it in the folder created by Flex Builder for the Chapter4 Flex project (see Figure 4-24).

When you export the Fireworks document, via File ➤ Export, be sure that you select MXML and Images in the Export dialog box. That way, you export the design you created in Firework not as an image but as an MXML file that Flex can read just as easily as if it were written in Flex Builder originally. All of the Flex components that you used in Fireworks to create the layout (for example, the three panels) are retained, and it will be possible to modify them in Flex Builder. The images that we used and modified will be compressed to the appropriate size and stored in a folder called images.

Figure 4-24. Use these settings in the Export dialog box.

Inside Flex Builder, if you select the fireworksLayout.mxml file, you will find that all of the work that you just did in Fireworks has transferred cleanly to Flex Builder. The images have been exported, complete with the effects; the transparency that you placed on the TextArea has been converted to a component property; and the positioning that you assigned to each component has been made into an absolute layout position (see Figure 4-25).

23. Open the file that was created in Fireworks (called fireworksLayout.mxml) from Flex Builder.

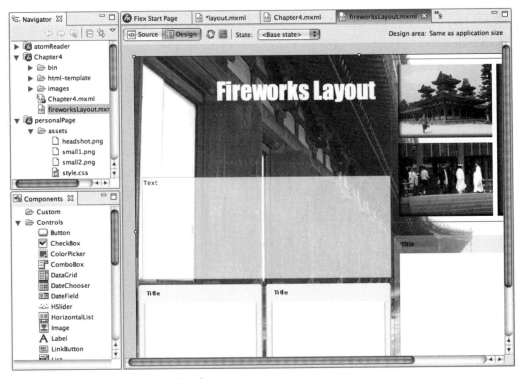

Figure 4-25. Components with an absolute layout

You will notice that we have not yet done a variety of tasks: we have not named our panels, added the TextArea components that will go into them, or applied CSS styling to our components. These things are best done with Flex Builder. Fireworks is principally a layout and graphics tool in the Flex application building process.

Summary

When it comes to the production process, Fireworks fits in best at the start of a project, when you are laying out the space for the components. It provides you with the alignment and resizing tools that make getting a tight, consistent layout easy to achieve. It also provides a good environment to make image modifications that are not possible to do in Flex Builder.

Building the layout of a Flex application in Fireworks allows you to take advantage of Fireworks' more advanced graphics capabilities, like alignment and cropping. Fireworks also lets you take advantage of filters, blend modes, and Photoshop Live Effects. Any image manipulation that you do in Fireworks will be exported as part of the original image. This means that browsers don't have to do any additional processing to display the effect.

Fireworks makes creating Flex application layouts easy by including a set of the most common Flex components. You can bring components such as combo boxes and panels into your design, position and scale them to fit with the layout, and then export them as a whole to Flex Builder.

In the next chapter, you'll be working with Photoshop and Illustrator to create custom skins for Flex components.

Chapter 5

FLEX WITH PHOTOSHOP AND ILLUSTRATOR

What we'll cover in this chapter:

- Bringing in Photoshop images as skins in Flex
- Scale 9
- Using Illustrator SWF features to simplify skinning

Files used in this chapter:

- skinImages (Button_upSkin.png, Button_overSkin.png, Button_downSkin.png, Button_disabledSkin.png)
- skinImages.css
- flex_skins.psd

We have looked at using CSS to control the visual look of your applications. Using CSS is the most effective and quickest way to have an impact, and there are many changes you can make through CSS. But there will always come a point where you want a more dramatic change—a point where you want to control not just the color and rounding of a button but also its shape and texture.

That is where skinning comes in. In a nutshell, skinning within Flex involves replacing the look of a component with an image. The idea is simple, but to execute it effectively often takes quite a bit of tweaking as each component is created by a series of smaller pieces or a representation for each state. The results can be very compelling, allowing you to create a distinct visual for your application.

Anatomy of a button

In Flex, when you look at a component, such as a button or a check box, you are really seeing an image that defines the visual appearance of the component in that state. For example, as you can see in Figure 5-1, a button consists of eight different states. In this chapter, we will replace the images for the first four. For simplicity, we won't be concerned with the button in selected mode.

Building skins in Photoshop

Let's begin by working with Photoshop to create a button that has a dramatically different appearance to a standard Flex button. The same process that we'll use with Photoshop can be used with alternative graphics programs such as Paint Shop Pro or The GIMP.

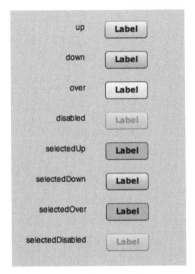

Figure 5-1. The eight states of a Button component

1. In Photoshop, create a new page. Set the size to be roughly the size of your button and set the background to be transparent (Figure 5-2). Give it the name Button.

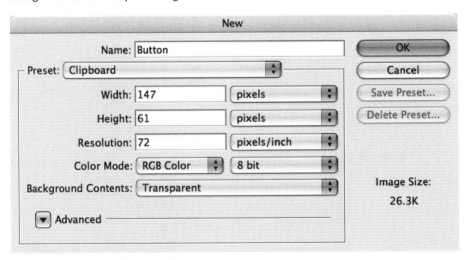

Figure 5-2. Create a new Photoshop file.

In this file we will draw how we want the up state to appear. This image will have the look of the button but not the text of the label that goes on top of it. We won't set the font here—we'll do that through CSS, which we'll add at the end.

To show how dramatic the change with skinning can be, the image that we have created is very different from the standard look of Flex. In this case, it has a hand-drawn feel (Figure 5-3).

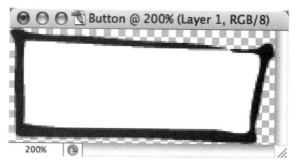

Figure 5-3. The up state of our button

This first image shows how the button will appear in the up state, or when the mouse is not on top of it.

2. Draw how you want your button's up state to look and save the image as a PNG-24 with the name Button_upSkin.

The naming of the images is very important here. The format is ComponentName_skinPart. This will let us automate the process of bringing the images into Flex Builder later. Note the capitalization.

3. Create a folder for the images called skinImages, and save the images to it.

We can now modify this Photoshop file to show what it will look like in its over state (when the mouse is over the button but not "pressing" it). We'll use the same image as a base so that it is in the same position. This prevents the button from moving a pixel or two over as it jumps to its over state. Figure 5-4 shows an example of how this button can look in its over state.

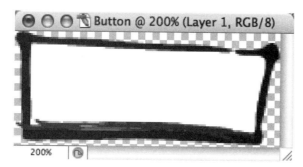

Figure 5-4. The over state of our button

4. Modify your image and save it as a PNG-24 called Button_overSkin.png.

93

5. Repeat this process to create and save images for the down state (Button_downSkin.png, Figure 5-5) and the disabled state (Button_disabledSkin.png, Figure 5-6).

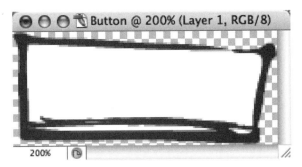

Figure 5-5. The down state of our button

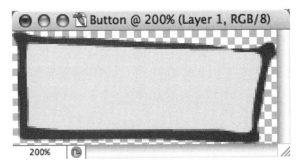

Figure 5-6. The disbaled state of our button

This should provide us with four images of the button as it would look through its different states.

The next step is to bring them into a button in Flex. To do this, we'll use CSS.

Connecting Photoshop skins

Start by switching from Photoshop to Flex so you can import your newly created button skins.

6. Open Flex Builder and create a new project called Skinning (File ➤ New ➤ Flex Project).

7. Bring the images into Flex Builder by selecting File ➤ Import.

This opens a dialog box that guides you through the import process for various file types. We are looking for Skin Artwork, which is found in the Flex folder (Figure 5-7).

8. Select Skin Artwork and click Next.

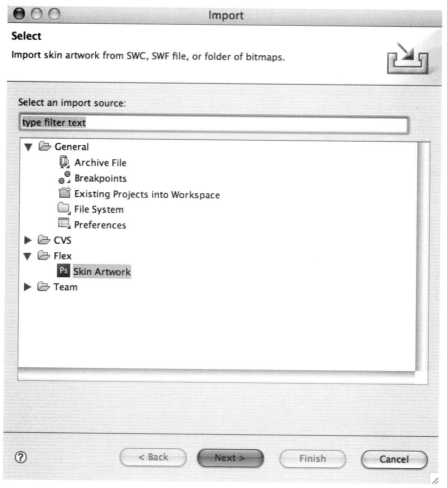

Figure 5-7. Importing a skin

9. Using the browse function, find the folder that holds the images that we just created (this folder should be called skinImages). Make sure that your current project is selected (Figure 5-8).

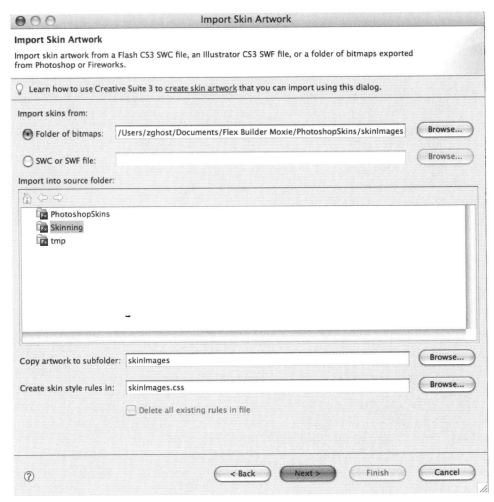

Figure 5-8. Import Skin Artwork

Let's take a quick look at what else the Import Skin Artwork wizard is doing at this point. The Copy artwork to subfolder field allows us to define the folder in our project structure that we want to copy the images to. You may want to specify an assets folder or keep it named skinImages. Also note that the wizard will create a CSS file in our project called skinImages.css.

10. Click Next and you'll see the screen in Figure 5-9.

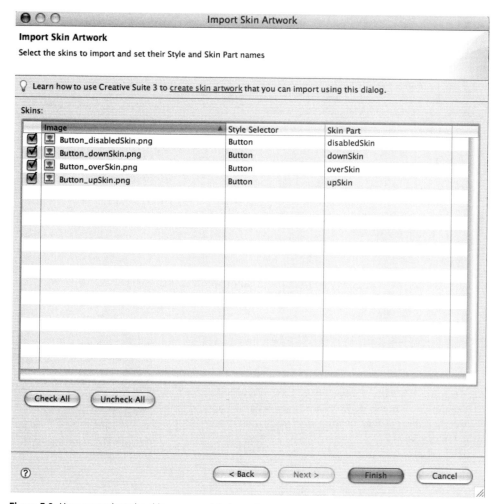

Figure 5-9. Here you select the skins you want to import.

Flex Builder is now creating a connection between the images that we created and the Button component. This connection is guided by the file names that we gave the images. If the file names are different, the Import Skin Artwork wizard will not recognize which image is associated with which component Skin Part. In this case, you can manually set this by double-clicking on either the Style Selector or Skin Part for each image.

11. Click Finish.

Once you click Finish, you'll see the CSS that Flex Builder automatically produced (Figure 5-10). The CSS first specifies which component it is referring to, in this case Button, then associates an image with each state through the Embed tag.

```
  1
  2  Button
  3  {
  4      disabledSkin: Embed(source="skinImages/Button_disabledSkin.png");
  5      downSkin: Embed(source="skinImages/Button_downSkin.png");
  6      overSkin: Embed(source="skinImages/Button_overSkin.png");
  7      upSkin: Embed(source="skinImages/Button_upSkin.png");
  8  }
```

Figure 5-10. Flex Builder creates this CSS for us.

We tell our Skinning.mxml to use this CSS file by adding the following code (in the same way we did in Chapter 2) to the MXML file:

```
<mx:Style source="skinImages.css"/>
```

Flex Builder created the Skinning.mxml file for us automatically when we created the project.

12. Add this code now.

With this code, any button component that we place in our project acquires the look that we just created (Figure 5-11).

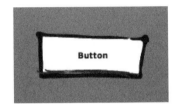

This button will automatically resize to match the size of your label, or the size that you manually give it. Have a look at how it changes when you expand it. To clearly show what is happening, we've stretched this one well beyond what you could expect from a button (Figure 5-12).

Figure 5-11. Skinned Button component

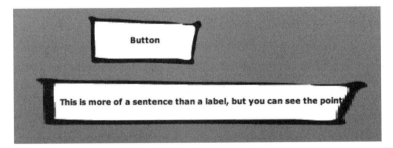

Figure 5-12. Skinned Button component, badly scaled

You can see some very bad pixelation as the corners and lines along the left and right sides have been stretched. This has happened because as the button scaled, the entire image scaled equally. Thankfully, there is a way to control how different parts of the image scale: the Scale 9 feature.

Scale 9

When we scale a component, we do not want it to scale equally. We want the sides to stretch up and down, but never to stretch sideways. We want the top and bottom to stretch sideways, but never to stretch vertically. As for the corners, we don't want them to stretch at all. This is what caused the pixelation in the previous example.

Let's go back to our button image in Photoshop. You can also open any one of the button PNG images that we created if that image is not handy.

1. In Photoshop, turn on the ruler. The shortcut for this is Ctrl+R (Windows) or Cmd+R (Mac). Make sure that the ruler is displaying pixels rather than inches. To change the ruler measurement units, right-click/Control-click on the ruler on the top or the left side of the image and select Pixels from the context menu that opens.

2. Drag out rules to define where the top, bottom, and sides of the button are by clicking on the ruler bar and dragging a rule out into position on the button (Figure 5-13).

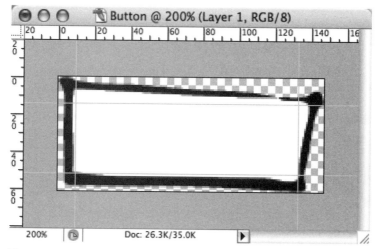

Figure 5-13. Our button in Photoshop with rulers defining Scale 9 areas

We do not have to do any slicing of this image into its sections—we merely need to know where the sections are. In this case, the left line is approximately 10 pixels in and the right is about 132. The top is about 14 pixels down from the top, and the bottom is 52 pixels down from the top. You can read these values off the rulers or, if you have the Info panel open in Photoshop, you can see the values for the rulers there. It is admittedly a bit difficult to see the edges on such an organic and skewed button, but the trick is to make sure that no part of the lines are inside the center box. The scaling of the lines in the wrong directions creates the most dramatic pixelation.

Now that we know where these lines should be, we can use CSS to control the scaling.

3. Using the numbers that you pulled from using the rulers in Photoshop, add the CSS between the brackets for the up state image, as shown in Figure 5-14.

```
Source    Design
1  /* CSS file */
2  Button
3  {
4      upSkin: Embed(source="skinImages/Button_upSkin.png",
5      scaleGridLeft="10",
6      scaleGridTop="14",
7      scaleGridRight="132",
8      scaleGridBottom="52");
9      overSkin: Embed(source="skinImages/Button_overSkin.png");
10     downSkin: Embed(source="skinImages/Button_downSkin.png");
11     disabledSkin: Embed(source="skinImages/Button_disabledSkin.png");
12 }
```

Figure 5-14. CSS for Scale 9

Since all the states of the button use the same scale values, you only assign the values to the upSkin property. You create scale values for the other states only if they differ from the upSkin.

4. Save the CSS, return to the MXML file, and refresh the view. Your buttons should now be scaling properly (Figure 5-15).

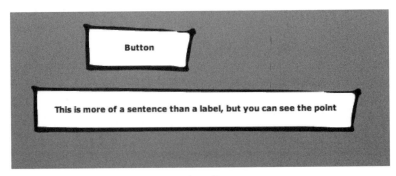

Figure 5-15. Our buttons are now properly scaling.

For more information on skinning Flex with CSS, especially if you are using Flex Builder 2, see "Designing Flex 2 Skins with Flash, Photoshop, Fireworks, or Illustrator" by Narciso Jaramilo at the Flex Developer Center website (http://www.adobe.com/devnet/flex/articles/flex_skins.html). This article shows the process of bringing in Flex skins and also includes a Photoshop file showing the default skins of Flex components (Figure 5-16).

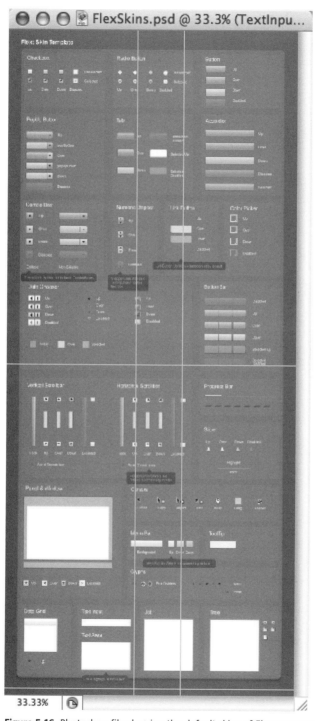

Figure 5-16. Photoshop file showing the default skins of Flex components

Using the CSS Design view

You can see how each component is created by using the CSS Design view. As Figure 5-17 shows, selecting the Design view in the CSS displays the default images as well as the newly embedded images for the specified component.

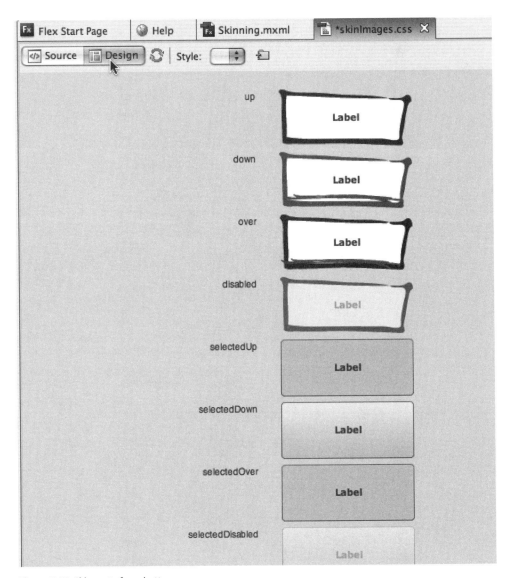

Figure 5-17. Skin parts for a button

1. Just for experimentation, create a new CSS file by choosing File ➤ New ➤ CSS File (Figure 5-18).

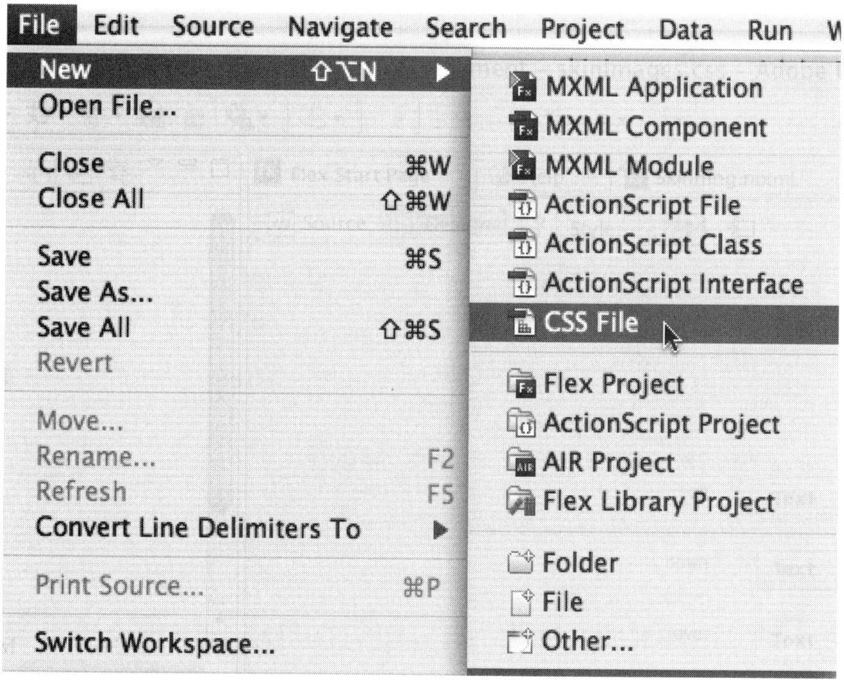

Figure 5-18. Create a new CSS file.

By entering an empty set of CSS for the component that you want to examine, you can see the default images that make up the component. For example, if you enter the CSS shown in Figure 5-19, you can see the images that make up a ComboBox component (Figure 5-20).

2. Type in the CSS as shown in Figure 5-19.

3. Select Design view.

Figure 5-19. CSS without attributes

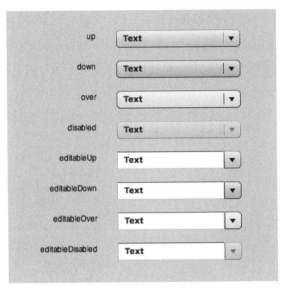

Figure 5-20. Skin parts for the ComboBox

Skinning Flex components in Illustrator using SWF files

Creating the skins for your Flex components in Illustrator follows a similar process but with some significant time-saving techniques available. You start in the same way, by creating the image for the component state, but the transition to Flex Builder is smoother. This is done by saving each state as a symbol and exporting the whole set as a .swf file. As with Photoshop, you use CSS to connect the symbols created in Illustrator and the components in Flex, but the information for the Scale 9 is contained within the symbols.

Let's walk through the process by creating a ComboBox skin within Illustrator.

1. Create a new document in Illustrator (Figure 5-21) and name it ComboBoxSkins.

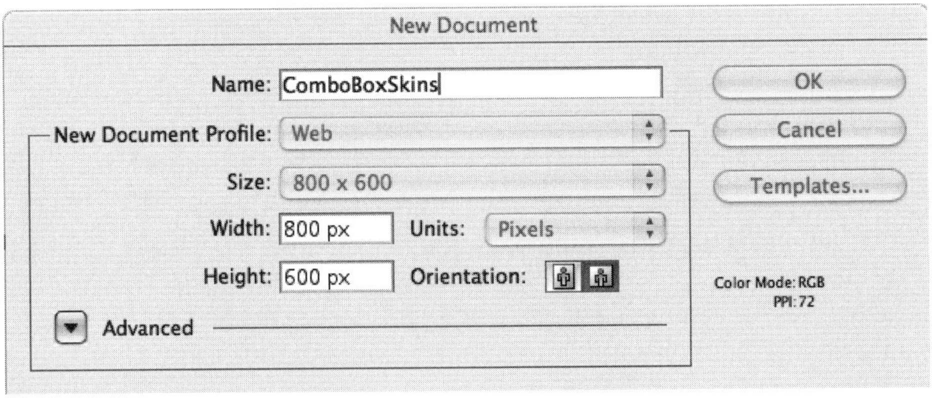

Figure 5-21. New Illustrator document

2. Draw an image of how you would like the up state of the ComboBox to look (Figure 5-22).

Figure 5-22. The up look for our ComboBox

3. Now convert this drawing to a symbol by dragging it onto the Symbols panel (Figure 5-23). To open the Symbols panel, press Shift+Ctrl+F11 (Windows) or Shift+Cmd+F11 (Mac). You can also open it by choosing Window ➤ Symbols from the main menu.

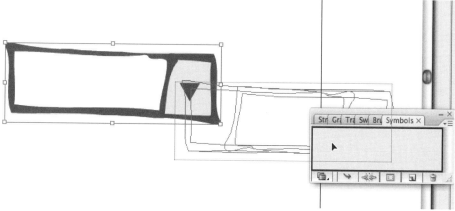

Figure 5-23. Converting the drawing to a symbol

When the symbol is being created, you will be prompted to define the symbol name (Figure 5-24); type in ComboBox_UpSkin. If you want to change the properties of the symbol later, you can open the properties by clicking the middle icon at the bottom of the Symbols panel between the Break Link to Symbol icon and the New Symbol icon.

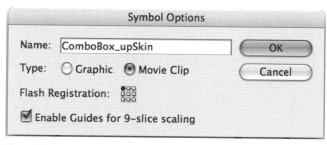

Figure 5-24. Naming our symbol

4. Use the same naming convention to name the symbol that we used for the Photoshop images (ComboBox_upSkin) and make sure that Enable Guides for 9-Slice Scaling is checked.

5. Double-click on the symbol so that you can modify the symbol, and most importantly, the Scale 9 guides.

6. Use the arrow to adjust the position of the Scale 9 guides (Figure 5-25).

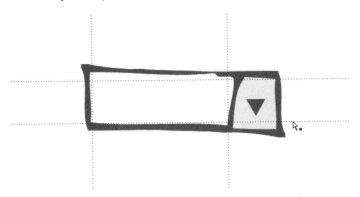

Figure 5-25. Adjust guides for 9-slice scaling

7. Now that you have established the Scale 9 guides, you can leave symbol-editing mode by clicking the arrow shown in Figure 5-26.

8. Create a duplicate of this symbol inside the symbol library by choosing Duplicate Symbol from the drop-down at the right of the Symbols palette (Figure 5-27).

Figure 5-26. Leaving symbol-editing mode

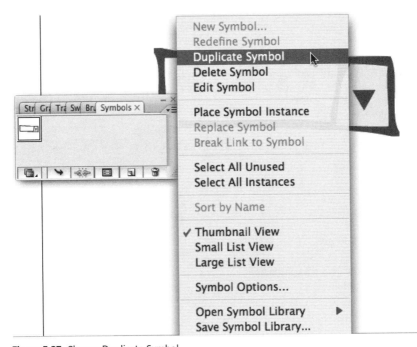

Figure 5-27. Choose Duplicate Symbol.

9. Change the name of the symbol so that it represents the down skin state (Figure 5-28).

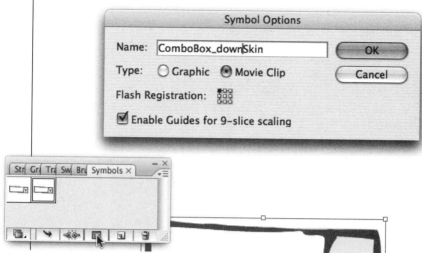

Figure 5-28. Use the Symbol Options dialog box to change the name.

10. Modify the symbol by double-clicking on it and adding some lines so that it has the look that you want when a user clicks on the ComboBox (Figure 5-29).

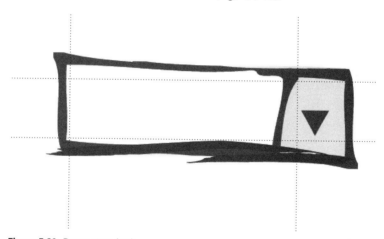

Figure 5-29. Down state look

11. Bring an instance of this new symbol onto the canvas.

12. Repeat steps 8–11 for each skin state that you want to modify. Remember to keep the naming consistent.

Once we have the symbols created for each of the states that we are planning on changing, we can export our symbols. Instead of saving each as an image, Illustrator allows us to keep things more organized by exporting all of the symbols as one SWF file.

13. Select File ➤ Export.

14. Select Flash (swf) from the Format pop-up list (Figure 5-30), and then click the Export button.

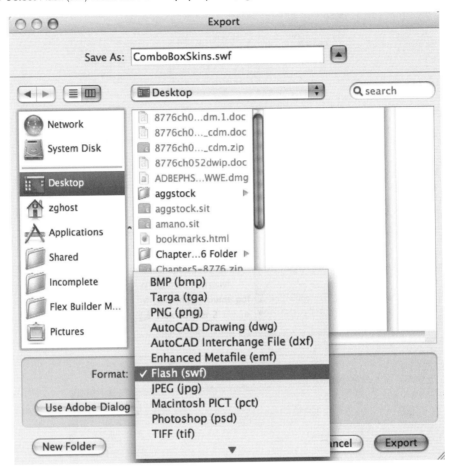

Figure 5-30. Choose the SWF format.

15. Use the default settings for the SWF (Figure 5-31). Click OK.

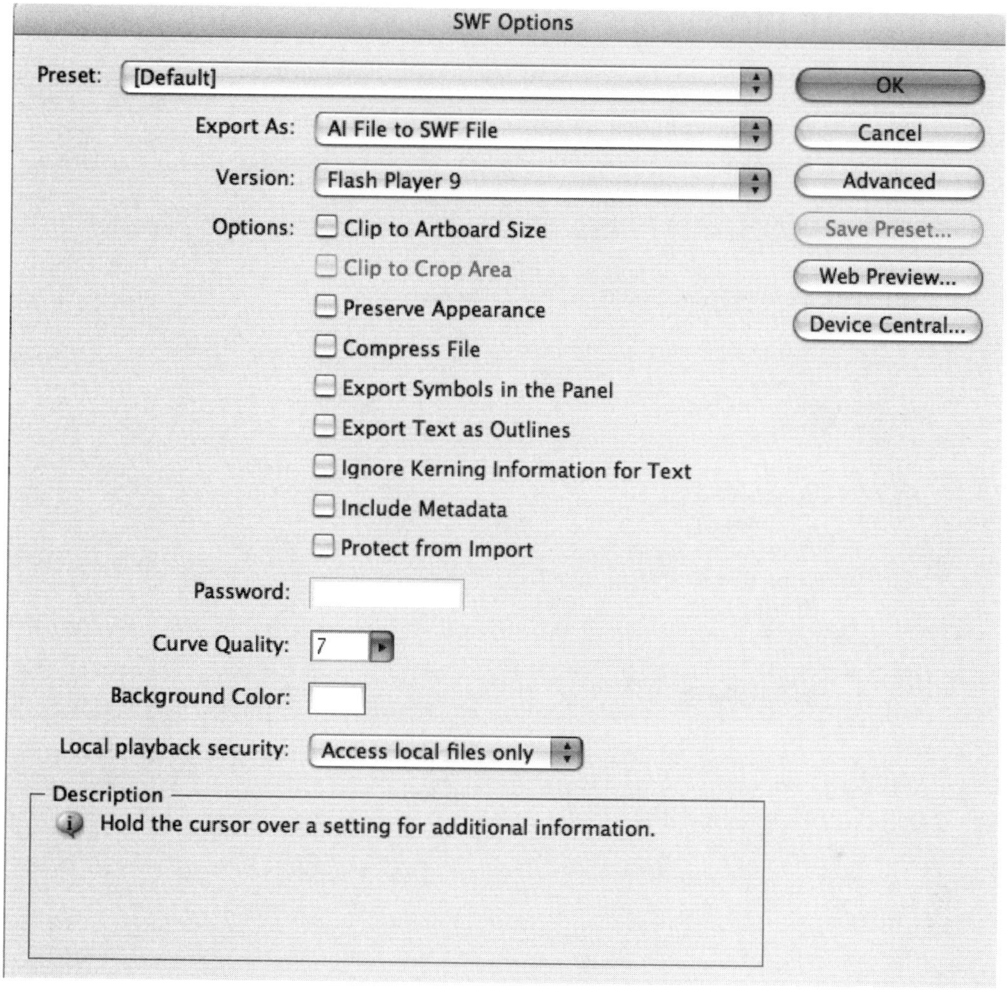

SWF Options

Preset: [Default]

OK

Export As: AI File to SWF File

Cancel

Version: Flash Player 9

Advanced

Options:
- [ ] Clip to Artboard Size

Save Preset...

- [ ] Clip to Crop Area

Web Preview...

- [ ] Preserve Appearance

Device Central...

- [ ] Compress File
- [ ] Export Symbols in the Panel
- [ ] Export Text as Outlines
- [ ] Ignore Kerning Information for Text
- [ ] Include Metadata
- [ ] Protect from Import

Password:

Curve Quality: 7

Background Color:

Local playback security: Access local files only

Description
ⓘ Hold the cursor over a setting for additional information.

Figure 5-31. Export settings

Importing the Illustrator skins into Flex Builder

In Flex Builder, we can now import the skins as we did the Photoshop images.

16. Select File ➤ Import in Flex Builder.

17. In the Import dialog box, select Skin Artwork, then click Next (Figure 5-32).

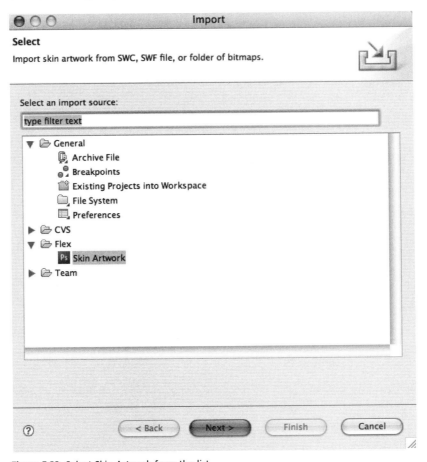

Figure 5-32. Select Skin Artwork from the list.

18. In the Import Skin Artwork dialog box (Figure 5-33), click the SWC or SWF file radio button under Import skins from, and browse to your ComboBoxSkins.swf file. Then, click Next.

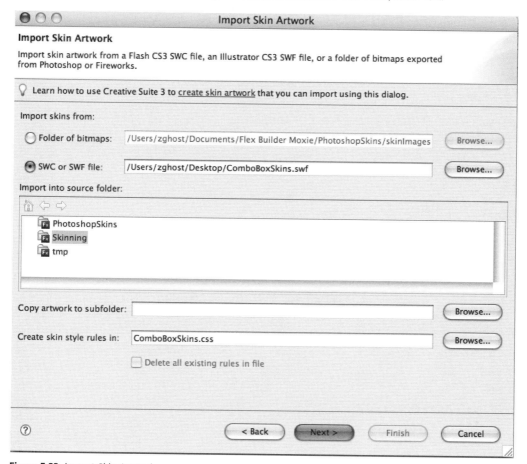

Figure 5-33. Import Skin Artwork

Once again you can see the symbols that we created are being recognized and linked to the appropriate component skin (Figure 5-34).

19. Click Finish.

The CSS that Flex Builder creates to link these symbols is similar to the CSS created for our Photoshop images, but it lists the name of the SWF and the symbol name. There is no need to add information for the Scale 9 as it is already included in the symbols (Figure 5-34).

```
1
2  ComboBox
3  {
4      disabledSkin: Embed(source="ComboBoxSkins.swf", symbol="ComboBox_disabledSkin");
5      downSkin: Embed(source="ComboBoxSkins.swf", symbol="ComboBox_downSkin");
6      overSkin: Embed(source="ComboBoxSkins.swf", symbol="ComboBox_overSkin");
7      upSkin: Embed(source="ComboBoxSkins.swf", symbol="ComboBox_upSkin");
8  }
```

Figure 5-34. This CSS links the skin state to our symbol.

All that is left is to link this CSS file to the MXML (Figure 5-35). Now any ComboBox that is added to this application will have the visual look that we have created.

```
1  <?xml version="1.0" encoding="utf-8"?>
2  <mx:Application xmlns:mx="http://www.adobe.com/2006/mxml" layout="absolute">
3
4  <mx:Style source="ComboBoxSkins.css"/>
5
```

Figure 5-35. Linking CSS to MXML

Summary

Although you can do a significant amount of modification to a design through CSS, when you need to have a dramatic change to the visuals of a component, you may have to do it through skinning. You can create skins for your components by either creating images for them (using Photoshop) or by creating a SWF file with the symbols included for each of the skin states (using Illustrator).

By skinning your components, you can change their texture and shape. Note that we have worked on the shape of the component but have not added text to it. Text is still controlled through CSS (as we did in Chapter 2).

In the next chapter you'll learn how Flex and Flash can be used together. This will involve bringing Flash animations into Flex Builder using a variety of techniques.

Chapter 6

FLEX BUILDER AND FLASH

What we'll cover in this chapter:

- Using a loader to import Flash animations
- Controlling Flash animations through Flex
- Creating dynamic skins for Flex components in Flash

Files used in this chapter:

- `octo.swf`
- `style.css`
- `FlexAndFlash.mxml`

Under the hood, Flash and Flex are closely related. Both work with ActionScript 3.0, both output to a SWF format, and both use Flash Player 9 to display their content. But they are very different in what they are good at. Flash started life as an animation program and developed more features as time went on, but animation is still one of its strongest points, and is more in line with what Adobe is intending it for in their modern suite of tools. Flex by contrast is really good at developing applications and the things that are associated with it—charting, handling data, and such. Sure, it can do animation, but the kinds of animation that Flex focuses on are things such as transitions that take place as menus expand, or items such as images scaling to different sizes in different states. We will be looking more closely at these effects and transitions when we build our photo gallery in Chapter 8.

There are three major ways to integrate Flash and Flex. The first is to use Flash to create skins and component animations. The second is to bring in complex timeline animations. And the third is to bring in Flash MovieClips that can be controlled in Flex. We will be looking at all three in this chapter.

Setting up to integrate Flash and Flex

Before we begin, we need to install two extensions that help integrate Flash and Flex. The first is the Flex Skin Design Extension for Flash. This extension simplifies the process for making Flex component skins in Flash. Extensions are also available for Photoshop, Illustrator, and Fireworks.

At the time of this writing, these extensions are available from the Adobe Labs site: http://labs. adobe.com/downloads/flex_sdext.html. These extensions can also be found with the files for this chapter in the code download for this book at www.friendsofed.com. To install the extensions, double-click on the .mxp file. This will open the Extension Manager and install the extension. Read and accept the disclaimer to complete the installation.

1. Install the Flex Skin Design Extensions for Flash.

The other extension that is important to install is the Flex Component Kit for Flash CS3 (also referred to as the Flash Integration Kit). This extension allows you to create Flex components from Flash MovieClips. The Flash Component Kit ships with Flex 3 and can be found in the /frameworks/flash-integration/ folder under the file name FlexComponentKit.mxp.

2. Install the Flex Component Kit.

3. You can now close the Extension Manager.

If Flash was open when you were installing the extensions, it will need to be restarted.

Creating Flex skins in Flash

It is not surprising that Flash is very effective at creating Flex skins. After all, Flash and Flex speak the same underlying technology (ActionScript 3.0), but Flash is designed to be more of a graphics and animation tool than Flex. By installing the Flex Skin Design Extension, we have installed a set of templates into Flash CS3 that aid us in creating Flex skins.

1. Open Flash CS3 and select Flex Skins on the Welcome screen (Figure 6-1).

The set of templates that are available cover a large variety of visual components. These templates hold the default skins for the individual components. The template flex_skins has a variety of components that you can change in a single file.

2. Open the template flex_skins (Figure 6-2).

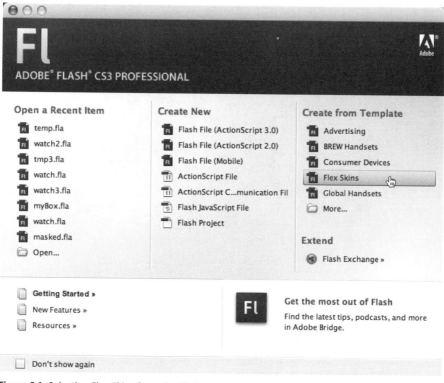

Figure 6-1. Selecting Flex Skins from the Welcome screen in Flash CS3

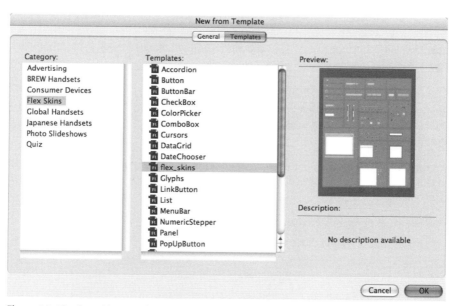

Figure 6-2. The flex_skins template selected in Flash CS3

117

In this file, you will find Flash MovieClips representing the skins of many Flex components (Figure 6-3). Each MovieClip contains the various states (up, down, over, and so forth) for that component.

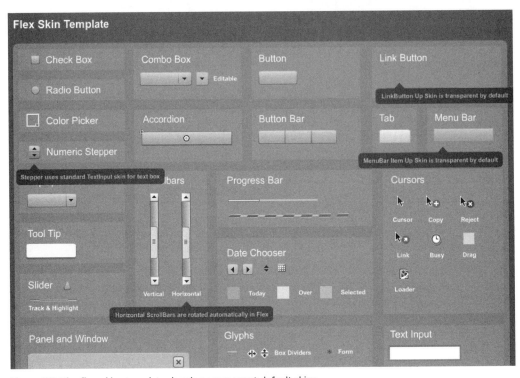

Figure 6-3. The flex_skins template showing component default skins

To change the skin of a component, open the MovieClip and change the graphics that make up the component. Begin by modifying the button component.

3. Double-click the button, which is a MovieClip named Button_skin, to edit the MovieClip.

In the button MovieClip you will find the four visual states of the button component spread out onto the timeline (Figure 6-4). Named keyframes represent each state. The dark gray dotted lines define the button for Scale 9 scaling.

The skins that are visible for each button state are a set of grouped graphics. To create your own skins, you can either modify these or delete the default graphics and create a new set. We will be using the second technique.

4. Delete the existing up state graphics from the art layer.

5. Draw in a new button up state using the Flash drawing tools.

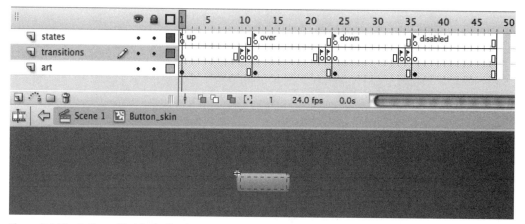

Figure 6-4. The Button_skin MovieClip showing keyframes representing button states

As you are drawing the new button up state, you are free to include any kind of texture, gradient, or visual style that is appropriate for your project. Keep in mind the Scale 9 guides so that your buttons scale correctly. For this example, create a button with a gradient fill and a second smaller button with an opposite gradient on top of it (Figure 6-5). The second opposite gradient provides a sense of depth and will be used in the second part of this example to show the use of tweens in buttons.

Figure 6-5. Button Up skin in Flash

It is useful to use this first button state as the starting point for all the other states.

6. Copy the button in the up state.

7. Go to the keyframe containing the down state (Frame 12).

8. Remove the default button visuals and paste in the button visuals you created for the up state. To ensure that the button visuals are pasted in the exact same x and y location as the up state button, choose Edit ➤ Paste in Place or press Ctrl+Shift+V (Windows) or Command+Shift+V (Mac).

9. Modify the visuals for the down state by rotating the smaller button 180 degrees. You can also add other changes such as making the outline of the button white (Figure 6-6).

119

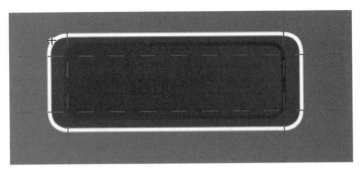

Figure 6-6. Button Over skin in Flash

10. Repeat the process of creating a new button state visual based on the up state (steps 7–9) for the down and disabled states. Feel free to experiment on the changes in these remaining states.

When we bring this Flash file into Flex, we will be able to use these images as the button skins for our project. Note that the type that goes on the button is not included within these skins. The typography is controlled through CSS once we are in Flex, as you saw in Chapter 2.

Adding animation

Since Flash is such a great animation tool, we can also use it to add animation to the button states. First let's create the animation for our transitions.

11. Select all of the frames in the up, over, and down states of the art layer. With these selected, in the Properties panel choose Shape from the Tween drop-down list (Figure 6-7).

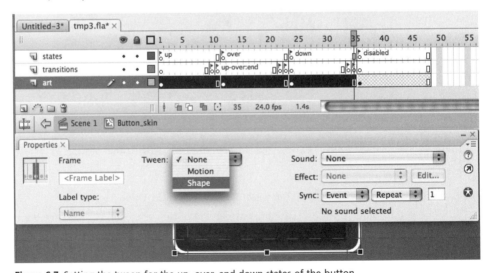

Figure 6-7. Setting the tween for the up, over, and down states of the button

This will create an animation that transitions from the up state to the over state to the down state that we created. Press Enter/Return to see the animations. Notice that the reversing of the gradient creates an interesting Flash effect on the button as it transitions from one state to the next.

120

The template file is already set up to make this easy for us to accomplish. Notice the layer above the art layer called transitions. This layer has two keyframes for each button state. For the up state, the keyframes are named up-over:start and up-over:end. These frames tell Flex which transition animation you want to create between the button states.

12. Drag the up-over:start keyframe to the start of the up state animation (Keyframe 1).

13. Repeat this for the other states, moving each keyframe ending in :start on the transitions layer start point of the transition (Figure 6-8).

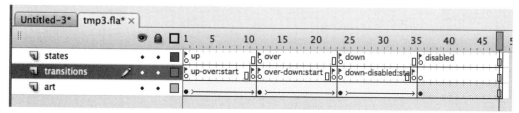

Figure 6-8. Moving the :start keyframes to the start of the animations for each button state

Bringing in a texture for a Panel

Different components have different kinds of graphics and different kinds of states, but the process for changing them is similar. You can use this technique to modify a wide range of components, importing images and textures into the visuals of a component.

14. As an example, double-click the Panel component to edit it (Figure 6-9).

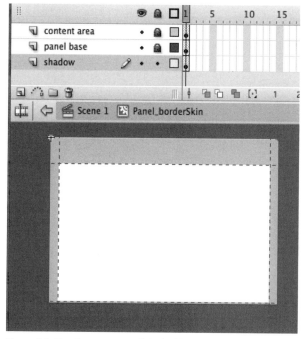

Figure 6-9. Panel component default skins

In Figure 6-9 you can see that the panel has some of the same characteristics as the button. It has the guiding lines for Scale 9 and is made up of multiple graphics. But it does not have multiple states, because a Panel does not change its appearance on rollover. To give this Panel a custom look, we are going to replace the gray of its background with a texture.

15. Import an image that you want to use as the Panel's background into the Library in Flash (File ➤ Import ➤ Import to Library), as shown in Figure 6-10. This allows you to select an image from your computer to import.

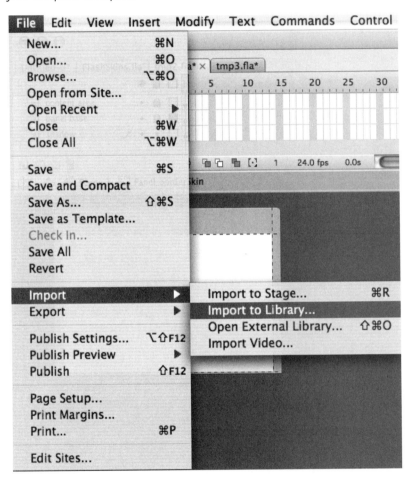

Figure 6-10. Importing an image into the Library in Flash

The imported image can now be used to replace the color on the background of the Panel.

16. Unlock both locked layers (panel base and content area), and select the background of the Panel. Open the Color panel (Figure 6-11).

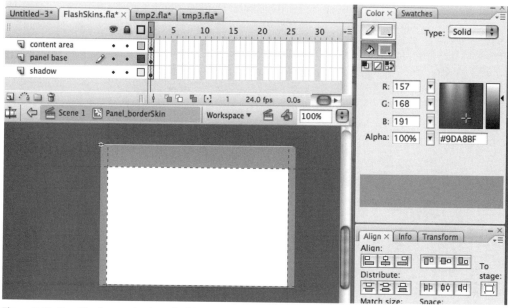

Figure 6-11. Panel background selected with Color panel open

17. Select Bitmap from the Type drop-down in the Color panel. The image that you imported into the library will appear as one of the swatches at the bottom of the Color panel (Figure 6-12). Select that swatch.

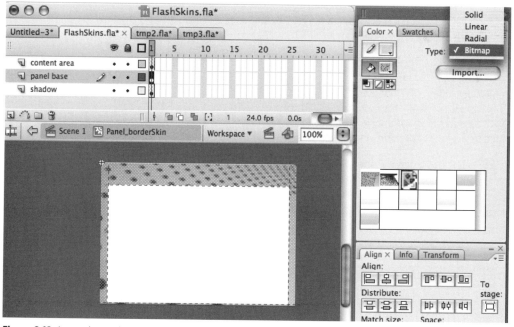

Figure 6-12. Importing an image into the Library in Flash

18. With the Color panel still open, select the content area layer and decrease the Alpha setting so that the background is more visible (Figure 6-13).

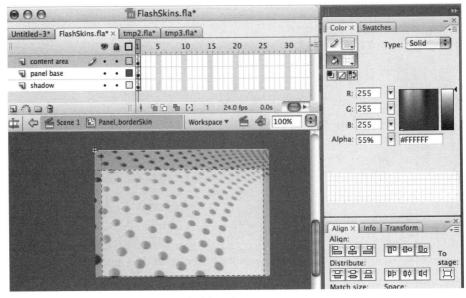

Figure 6-13. Content area with decreased Alpha value

Going from Flash to Flex

Once you have modified the skins of the Flex components in Flash, you can publish the file.

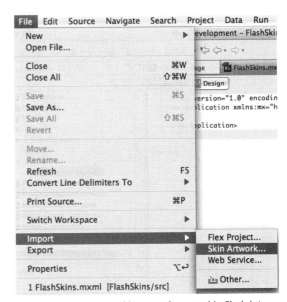

19. Save the Flash file as Skins.fla and publish the Flash file (File ➤ Publish).

Publishing the file creates two files: flex_skins.swf and flex_skins.swc. The SWC file format is an archive file that Flex can open to access the skins that we created.

20. If it is not yet open, open Flex Builder and create a new project (File ➤ New ➤ Flex Project) called FlashSkins.

21. Import the skins into Flex by selecting File ➤ Import ➤ Skin Artwork (Figure 6-14).

Figure 6-14. Importing skin artwork created in Flash into Flex

22. In the Import Skin Artwork dialog box, under Import skins from:, select SWC or SWF file: and browse to find the flex_skins.swc file that we created earlier (Figure 6-15). Click Next.

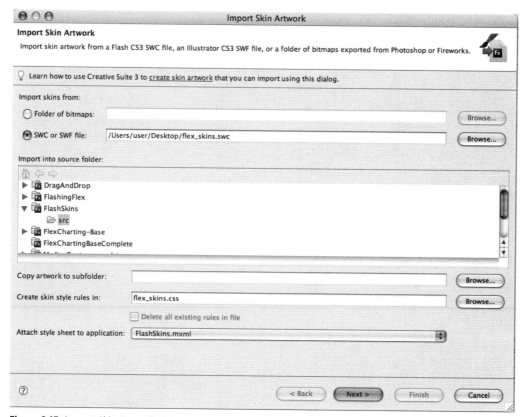

Figure 6-15. Import Skin Artwork dialog box, step 1

The next dialog box shows a list of all the Flex skins that were in the SWC.

23. Click Uncheck All and select the skins that you modified in Flash—in this example, Button_skin and Panel_borderSkin (Figure 6-16). Click Finish.

The skins that we created in Flash are now in the Flex project. Notice that the flex_skins.swc file now appears in the src folder of the Flex project along with the MXML file and a CSS file called flex_skins.css. The CSS file opens automatically. This CSS controls the connection between the SWC file and the panels.

125

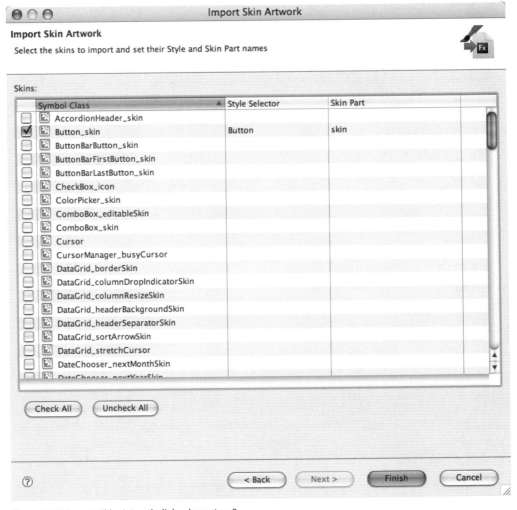

Figure 6-16. Import Skin Artwork dialog box, step 2

24. Open the FlashSkins.mxml file. Pull out a Button and a Panel component and place them as shown in Figure 6-17. Run the project.

You will notice that the skins that we created in Flash are now used to display the components. The animations on the button are also visible on rollover. It's interesting that the animations we created for rollover are automatically reversed for rollout.

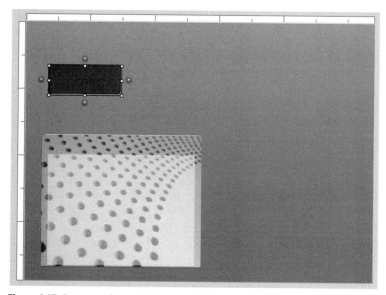

Figure 6-17. Button and Panel with custom skins in Flex Builder

Importing Flash animations into Flex

The simplest way to import Flash content into Flex is to use the SWFLoader. The SWFLoader is a component that brings in Flash content in much the same way an Image component brings in a .jpg. For this example, a SWF file called octo.swf is provided with the files for this chapter. This Flash file contains an animation by designer Mark Okon. It contains the kind of complex, cell-based animation that is easy in Flash but difficult in Flex.

1. Pull out a SWFLoader component from the Controls folder in the Components panel and place it next to the Button and Panel that were created earlier (Figure 6-18). Give the SWFLoader an ID of octo.

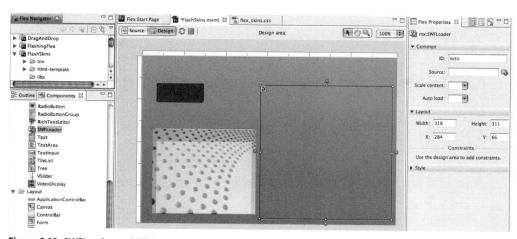

Figure 6-18. SWFLoader on MXML

You are going to want the SWF file to be kept with the rest of your files for the project.

2. Drag the octo.swf file from the location where you saved it into the File Navigator panel in the src folder (Figure 6-19).

3. Enter the name of the file in the Source field in the SWFLoader properties.

4. Run the project (Figure 6-20).

You will notice that the Flash file has been loaded into the SWFLoader and scaled to fit. You can turn the scaling off by setting the Scale content property to false. You can also see that the animation of the Flash file is brought in but not the background. This lets your animation fit more effectively with the Flex application.

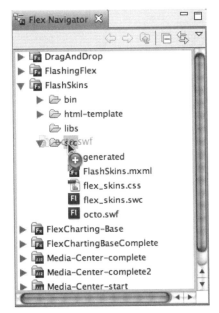

Figure 6-19. Copying octo.swf into our project

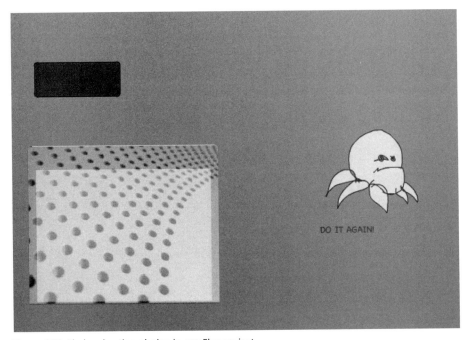

Figure 6-20. Flash animation playing in our Flex project

The buttons in the Flash file also still work to affect the content in the Flash file. So the Do It Again! button in octo.swf still replays the animation if it is inside Flex. But there is little interaction between the Flash animation and Flex. Using this method, we cannot, for example, use a Flex Button to set a property in the Flash animation. To create this kind of deeper interlacing we need to use the Flex Component Kit (also known as the Flash Integration Kit) that we installed at the start of this chapter.

Integrating Flash and Flex in a deeper way

In the files for this chapter you'll find a Flash FLA file called watch.fla.

1. Copy this file to your desktop and open it in Flash.

In the Library of the file is the kind of MovieClip that you might expect to be used in an online store. The MovieClip contains four images of a watch at different angles, each on its own labeled keyframe (Figure 6-21).

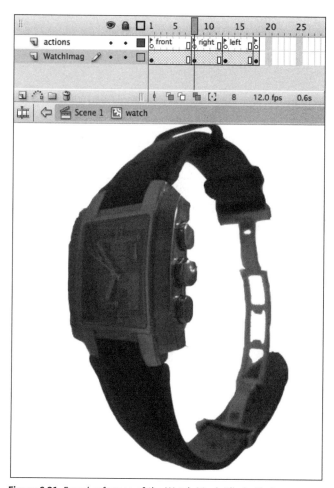

Figure 6-21. Four keyframes of the Watch MovieClip in Flash

Our goal in this example is to bring the MovieClip into Flex and have it respond to Flex events. In this way a Flex event, such as a button click or state change, can affect the angle of the watch.

Adding the Flex Component Kit has created a new command in Flash: Make Flex Component (Figure 6-22).

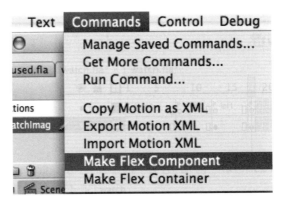

Figure 6-22. Make Flex Component command, added by the Flex Component Kit

It is this command that lets us create the watch MovieClip as a Flex component and modify it through Flex events.

2. Select the Watch MovieClip in the Flash Library and select the command Make Flex Component (Commands ➤ Make Flex Component).

This does a series of things. First, it changes the frame rate to 24 fps, the frame rate at which Flex operates, if it is different. It also turns Export SWC on and imports FlexComponentBase into the Flash Library. Publishing this file now creates a Watch.swc file along the with SWF and HTML files. It is this SWC file that we'll use to import the Watch into Flex Builder.

3. Publish the Flash file (File ➤ Publish).

To bring the Watch into Flex Builder, we need to create a library path for it.

4. In Flex Builder, create a new project called FlashingFlex (New ➤ Flex Project).

5. For this project, open the project's properties (Project ➤ Properties).

6. In the Properties dialog box, select Flex Build Path and then Library Path (Figure 6-23).

7. Click Add SWC and browse to find the SWC file we published in Flash (Watch.swc).

8. Click OK to finish connecting the Watch to the Flex file.

The Watch MovieClip can now be used as a Flex component.

9. Bring out a Panel that will be used to hold the Watch. The Panel needs to be 380 pixels by 490 pixels to hold the Watch in its original scale, but the Watch can also be scaled if needed.

10. In the Source view, begin to type the MXML tag for the watch. Notice that as you begin to type <wa the code hint feature offers the rest of the MXML tag for the Watch (Figure 6-24). The tag should read <local:watch id="theWatch"/>.

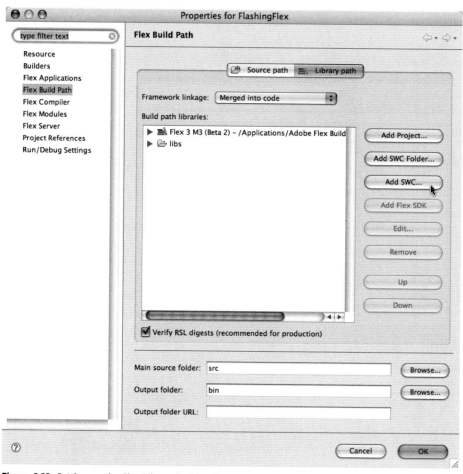

Figure 6-23. Setting up the Flex Library build path

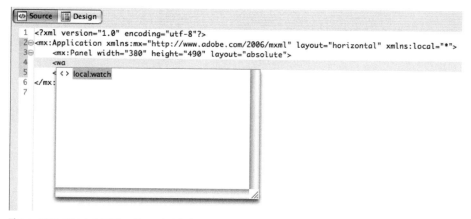

Figure 6-24. Watch MXML with code hinting

Jumping back to the Design view, you can see the Watch in its position (Figure 6-25).

Figure 6-25. Watch component in the Panel

11. Add a ControlBar from the Layout folder in the Components panel. Place four Buttons on the ControlBar named Front, Right, Left, and Side (Figure 6-26).

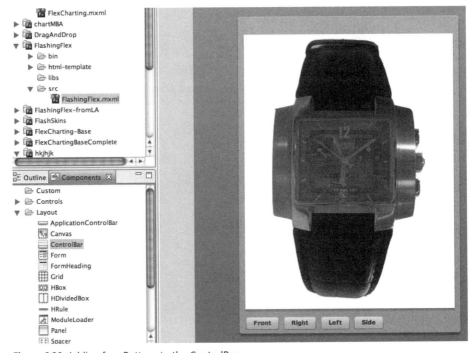

Figure 6-26. Adding four Buttons to the ControlBar

We'll use these four buttons to control the view of the watch. Let's create a function that essentially runs the gotoAndStop code that is used in Flash but made to work in Flex. Figure 6-27 shows the function.

```
<mx:Script>
<![CDATA[
    private function goToLabel(label:String): void
    {
        theWatch.gotoAndStop(label);
    }
]]>
</mx:Script>
```

Figure 6-27. Function for controlling the current frame in Watch

12. Copy this code into your MXML Source view. When called, this function tells the Watch to go to the frame label that is used.

13. For each of the buttons, call the function from the OnClick event with the appropriate label. For the front button, set OnClick to goToLabel('front'); for the side button, set it to goToLabel('side'); for the left button, set it to goToLabel('left'); and for the right button, set it to goToLabel('side'). Give each button an ID that is the same as its label. Once you've done that, test your movie. Figure 6-28 shows the application in action.

Figure 6-28. Final application

Summary

With that function, Flex has taken control of what was originally Flash content. You are not limited to button clicks for this kind of interaction. Any Flex event, such as a state change or a change in data, can call a function, and so cause a change in content originally created in Flash.

In the next chapter we look more closely at programming with ActionScript in Flex Builder.

Chapter 7

ACTIONSCRIPT IN FLEX

What we'll cover in this chapter:

- Overview of object-oriented programming
- ActionScript 3.0 key concepts

We have already seen that building Flex applications often involves a combination of components and ActionScript. We have tried to keep the ActionScript in our examples simple and clear, but as the interaction becomes more complex, so does the ActionScript involved. Now is a good time to look at ActionScript 3.0 and to familiarize yourself with some of the ActionScript that we will be working with in the next few chapters. The intention of this chapter is not to make you a developer or to teach programming, but to give you an understanding of how ActionScript works and relates to the components. This will ultimately make you a better Flex designer.

Overview

Flex uses ActionScript 3.0. This is the current version of ActionScript and a significant jump in capability from ActionScript 2. It is more powerful, can use larger data sets, and is much faster (up to 10 times faster) than previous versions. In many ways, ActionScript 3.0 provides greater scope in the creation and development of more complex Flex applications. ActionScript 3.0 is an object-oriented programming (OOP) language, and before we can start talking about ActionScript we need to have a general understanding of the meaning of object-oriented programming.

What is object-oriented programming?

Object-oriented programming isn't as scary as it sounds; it's just a popular way of writing programs, and is the style that's used in ActionScript 3.0. At its most basic level, it means that rather than writing one long program to deal with a specific problem, you break that problem down into chunks and write smaller blocks of code (objects) to address each part of the problem. There are many benefits to OOP, but there are two obvious ones that I'll mention here. First of all, although you're writing an application to address a specific problem, because the code objects are separate functional blocks, you can use them again in other applications. For example, you may create a simple object for a calculator application that takes a set of values and returns the average. If you were then to create, say, a graphing application, you could use the same "Average" object in your new application without having to program it again from scratch. Second, it's easy to update or modify object-oriented code because you can make changes to a specific object without affecting the rest of the application. Those are just two examples, but you get the idea that OOP is a useful approach to follow.

If this definition is not clear now, don't worry—as we continue it will become clearer. Just remember to come back and read it again if you need to, once you are done reading the rest of the chapter.

There is one other key OOP concept that you should know early on: the difference between classes and objects. Let's take an example of a schematic you've designed to manufacture a toy rubber duck. The schematic, or blueprint, is the *class* for the rubber duck. It describes what the rubber duck will be, and is the single template for creating unlimited numbers of rubber ducks. Each rubber duck that rolls off the production line is an *object* based on the rubber duck class. In programming terms, each of these rubber duck objects is described as being an "instance" of the rubber duck class.

What is ActionScript?

ActionScript is the object-oriented programming language used by Adobe Flex to achieve complex interactions and animations. ActionScript is an important part of any application that leverages the Flash platform. This is why designers should concern themselves at the very least with its importance and its purpose.

ActionScript started as a scripting language for Flash ActionScript 1 to enable a tighter control of animations, and was well received by the community and widely adopted by designers and developers, motivating Macromedia and then Adobe to push it further and further with every release of Adobe Flash. In time ActionScript 2 was introduced, being more compliant with OOP principles and enabling even more control and better performance until the release of ActionScript 3.0.

One more important point to mention is that the Flash Player was completely rewritten by Adobe to work with ActionScript 3.0, thus making a giant leap in performance compared to ActionScript 1 and 2. After the release of the Flash Player 9, a new virtual machine (VM) was introduced in the Player just for applications using ActionScript 3.0, but the old VM is still there for backward compatibility in order to run applications using ActionScript 1 and 2. Don't worry if you're not sure what a VM is—it sounds complicated but it's very simple. Essentially, a VM is like an interpreter, and it means that you just need to write your applications in one language, ActionScript, and the Flash Player's VM will translate that into code that the computer it's running on understands. You don't need to know if the user is running Windows, Mac OS X, Linux, or whatever—the VM will make sure your code runs on that system without a hitch.

Explaining the differences between versions of ActionScript is beyond the scope of this book, but the differences are mostly evolutionary in nature, and for someone new to it, is a good idea to learn ActionScript in its current incarnation as 3.0.

To understand ActionScript, you must familiarize yourself with a number of concepts; it will be nearly impossible to explain it all in one chapter. The goal here is not to convert you into a developer but to demystify some of the key concepts, allowing you to better understand Flex and communicate more efficiently with a developer.

What is MXML?

Flex in addition to ActionScript also includes a markup language named MXML that is based on XML. Its purpose is to simplify the process of creating interfaces and layouts in Flex. There is no canvas onto which you can draw something directly in Flex as you would in Flash, and it would be tedious to have to create a graphical user interface (GUI) programmatically entirely in ActionScript. This is when MXML comes to the rescue, allowing you to quickly create an interface by declaring a few tags.

MXML is very powerful but is sometimes underestimated. If there is one aspect of Flex I'd encourage designers to learn it is MXML. It will give you as much flexibility with layout as you'd obtain by learning HTML—and perhaps even more.

A fact that is often forgotten is that below the surface, all MXML tags are actually ActionScript classes (remember the rubber ducks!), and Flex transforms all of this MXML into ActionScript in the background, enabling you to just work with simple MXML tags without having to learn the more complex ActionScript behind it . . . most of the time. Because the MXML tags are prebuilt ActionScript classes, they only let you create things based on those classes, and they only let you interact with those classes in the way that the Adobe engineers programmed them. If you want to do anything out of the ordinary, you'll need to go back to the ActionScript to add extra functionality.

Some key ActionScript concepts

This section will explore some of the key ideas and techniques that are used in ActionScript. They are interrelated and come together like Lego pieces to help you get the right interaction from your applications.

Understanding packages

A package is a way to organize a group of classes in a directory. Remember that classes are like templates—little functional blocks of code that do something—and they are often stored in separate files. If you are working with several files with a common goal, you will want to naturally organize them somehow, perhaps grouping them into a folder or "package" (hence the name). This way, you can share that group of files easily by transporting just one folder.

You would also like to give your package a descriptive and unique name, one that will give you a good idea of what those files do and at the same time not conflict with another package. A good way to avoid a name conflict is to use domain names, which are unique; for example, I own a domain name, lordalex.org, and no one else can have that domain.

A name like myPackage would easily come in conflict with someone else's unless you use the domain name. To use the domain name, create a directory named org. Inside that directory, create another one (I use the name lordalex) and inside this folder place myPackage. Notice we use the domain in reverse, i.e., org is before lordalex.

The nesting of folders is this fashion ensures that the files don't conflict with anyone else's. The resulting structure looks like this:

    org/lordalex/myPackage/MyClass.as

In ActionScript, to create a package you need to define it as shown in Figure 7-1.

```
package org.lordalex.myPackage {

    class MyClassHere {
            // some statement
    }
}
```

Figure 7-1. Package definition

Classes and objects

Let's revisit the difference between classes and objects in a little more detail. A class is a fundamental part of OOP; it is the blueprint for another entity we will become familiar with called an object. These two concepts are intimately related. In real life we see classes all the time. Say you find yourself in the supermarket looking at the fruit section, looking at a pile of apples. There are many of them, but they all have the same or similar characteristics. Their skin is red, they are almost round, and so forth. You can recognize them as apples, because you know the characteristics of an apple. You just identified an object (the apple) of the class Apple (its blueprint).

A class in programming is the blueprint from which objects are created. An object is an instance of a class; it is an individual unit capable of receiving and sending messages, processing data on its own, and interacting with other objects.

Another example in real life are dogs; individual dogs can be thought of as objects. There are many of them but they all belong to the class Dog.

The basic structure of a class is simple. Here we have a class Dog, enclosed in the package myAnimals. You define a class by using the word class followed by the name you want to give it.

It is important to remember that class names always start with an uppercase letter and that every class generally has a "constructor," which is a function that shares the same name as the class. The constructor is a function that executes by default the second you create an instance of a class (Figure 7-2).

```
package org.lordalex.myAnimals
{
    public class Dog
        function Dog ()
        {
            trace("I am the constuctor for the Dog class," +
            " I execute as soon as a new instance of a dog is created");
        }
}
```

Figure 7-2. Class definition with a constructor

An object is instantiated through the use of the word new, as shown in Figure 7-3.

```
public var myDog:Dog = new Dog();
```

Figure 7-3. Instantiation of the class Dog

Methods

When we talk about methods in ActionScript, we essentially are talking about functions. These functions are encapsulated pieces of code that do a specific task and may or may not return a value after doing these actions.

You identify these encapsulated pieces of code with the word function followed by the method name, and enclose whatever action you want to create within braces ({}). Let's expand on the Dog class by adding a method named bark(), which will simulate our Dog barking (Figure 7-4).

The word public is the access modifier. We will be discussing this a bit later in this chapter, but for the moment simply assume that it needs to be there.

```
public function bark():void
{
    trace("woof! woof!");
}
```

Figure 7-4. The bark() method

When we call this function, it immediately executes the line trace("woof! woof!");. trace is a command in ActionScript that helps debug your applications by printing information to the console in Flex when you click the Debug button.

Methods are very important because they constitute the body of a class. They work as small pieces of code that break the functionality of a class into manageable pieces.

As I mentioned earlier, a function may or may not return a value after it finishes executing its task. In our case, we are not returning a value of any kind. We denote this with a colon and the word void

139

right after the closing parenthesis after the function name. However, functions can also take in values, process those values, and return a new value.

Keep in mind that all methods you create must have a return type, even if your function is not intended to return any value, as in our example. You define a return type after the function name, also known in programming lingo as a function's *signature*. If you forget, Flex Builder will highlight this as a compile-time error and will not compile properly.

It is worth mentioning that any variables you declare inside a function are created and destroyed immediately after the function is done executing.

For example, we are going to teach our Dog how to add by telling him two values and making him tell us the result. To achieve this, create the function shown in Figure 7-5.

```
private function sum(num1:Number, num2:Number):Number
{
        var newValue:Number = num1 + num2;
        return newValue;
}
```

Figure 7-5. The sum() method

Notice inside the parentheses our function expects two values of type Number. We must tell the function what sort of value to expect. Also, our function includes Number after the colon, which means that this function returns a new value and that it is of the numerical type. Finally, return is there to tell the function to send back the result of our sum.

Just as you cannot go without specifying a function's return type (unless you use void), you will need to use the return statement in the method itself.

Access modifiers

Access modifiers might sound very alien, but they are just a set of keywords that you use when creating packages, classes, functions, and variables to control how they are accessed. These keywords are as follows:

- public means the class can be accessed openly and without restrictions.
- private means just that: the class and its contents are not available to other classes.
- internal means the class can be accessed from classes in its own package—a sort of semi-public.
- protected works like a semi-private: members are only available to subclasses.

These allow developers to control the access they wish to provide to their packages, classes, functions, or variables in their code.

I created a new package named myAnimals; inside it I created a simple class, Dog. If you look closely, the properties legs and tail have been set as private variables. The logic here is that I created a blueprint for what a Dog is (see Figure 7-6); we know Dogs have four legs and one tail, and I do not want anyone changing those values (after all, we wouldn't want a dog with six legs and two tails, would we?).

Also, there is a private method, breathe(). This function should be used internally in the class. I could have a timer that would call this method automatically every two seconds inside the class to simulate the dog breathing. This is a perfect example of a method you'd want to keep private, as opposed to bark() and sit(), which are public because unlike breathing (which is something that should be regulated internally by the object itself), you want to teach your Dog to sit or bark on command.

```
package org.lordalex.myAnimals
{
    public class Dog
    {
        //these are class private properties available to this class only
        private var legs:Number = 4;
        private var tail:Number = 1;

        function Dog()
        {
         trace("I am the constructor for the Dog class, " +
               "I execute as soon as a new instance of a dog is created");
        }
        //
        public function bark():void
        {
            trace("woof! woof!");
        }
        //
        public function sit():void
        {
            trace("dog is sitting")
        }
        // private method breathe
        private function breathe():void
        {
            trace("the dog is breathing");
        }
        //
        private function sum(num1:Number, num2:Number):Number
        {
            var newValue:Number = num1 + num2;
            return newValue;
        }
    }
}
```

Figure 7-6. Package with class and methods

Variables arrays and collections

Variables are special containers where you can store information to be later used in your program. At their simplest, they contain only one value at time, but there are more complex variable types such as arrays that can contain multiple values. We'll cover those a little further, but for the moment let's take a closer look at simple variables.

We create a variable as shown in Figure 7-7.

```
var myFirstVariable:int = 5;
```

Figure 7-7. A simple variable

The keyword var means we are creating a variable. You can name your variable whatever you like as long it follows these requirements:

- The name must not contain any spaces.
- The first character must be a letter, underscore (_), or dollar sign ($).
- Each subsequent character must be a letter, number, underscore, or dollar sign.
- The instance name must be unique.

It is good practice to give variables meaningful names that help illustrate their purpose in your code. You also need to define what type value your variable will be storing. To define the variable type, append a colon after the variable name and enter the variable type, for example, string, number, or int (for integer). In our example, we want to store integer values. Then you can assign a value to your variable using the equal sign. Close the statement with a semicolon.

You can also assign the content of one variable to another, as shown in Figure 7-8.

```
var myFirstVariable:int = 5;

var mySecondVariable:int = myFirstVariable;
trace (mySecondVariable); // output is 5
```

Figure 7-8. Passing a variable by value

In programming lingo, we call this "passing a variable by value." This means that even if you delete myFirstVariable, it will not have an effect on mySecondVariable. More complex variables, such as arrays, are passed by reference. Let's have a closer look at arrays.

Arrays are a special type of container that can generally hold multiple values ordered by an index. In real life you have used arrays without knowing it. When you write a grocery list, for example, your list contains a number of items; you can think of groceries as the name of the array that holds the items you need to purchase.

It would look something like this:

groceries:

- Milk
- Eggs
- Beef
- Chicken
- Carrots

We use arrays in programming for the same reason you'd create a grocery list: it's convenient. You create your grocery list so you can easily iterate all the items and mark them off as you find them in the supermarket.

Figure 7-9 shows how our list would look in ActionScript.

```
public var groceries:Array = new Array("Milk", "Eggs", "Beef", "Chicken", "Carrots");
```

Figure 7-9. The array groceries

To access the first element in the groceries array, use the name of the array as an index (Figure 7-10). Notice that arrays in ActionScript are zero based, which means [0] and not [1] is the first element of the array.

```
trace (groceries[0]); // output is Milk
trace (groceries[3]); // output is Chicken
```

Figure 7-10. Tracing the array groceries

To change a value on this list, we also use the array index (Figure 7-11).

```
groceries[3] = "Turkey" // this replaces the value "Chicken" with "Turkey"
```

Figure 7-11. Changing the array groceries

Another advantage of using arrays is the methods we can use to work with the data they hold. One such method is Array.length, which returns the number of values contained in the array. Figure 7-12 shows an example.

```
trace(groceries.length); // output 5
```

Figure 7-12. Getting the length of an array

You can also pass an array value to another array, but the results are a bit different (Figure 7-13).

```
// copying a variable passes the data by reference not value
public var groceriesCopy:Array = groceries;

groceriesCopy[2] = "Strawberries";

trace(groceries); //output is Milk,Eggs,Strawberries,Chicken,Carrots
trace(groceriesCopy);// output is Milk,Eggs,Strawberries,Chicken,Carrots
```

Figure 7-13. Creating a copy of an array

In Figure 7-13, we created a copy of our groceries array. Within the copied array, we then changed the third value, Beef, to Strawberries. When we use trace to look at the values of our arrays, we see that both the copy and the original array have changed. This is different from the earlier example with a simpler variable. In that example, myFirstVariable can be changed or even deleted without affecting mySecondVariable. Why the difference? The answer is that some complex variables in ActionScript are passed by reference and not by value, thus pointing to the values of the variable rather than creating a duplicate and independent set of values.

There is now also a more advanced form of arrays: the ArrayCollection. Collections, which are ActionScript 3.0 classes, are unique to Flex. In simple terms, this is a class that envelops the Array class, adding a number of convenient ways to interact with the values of the array. Explaining arrays and collections in detail is beyond the scope of this chapter, but it is important to at least know they exist. The ArrayCollection class exists for convenience. Array has a number of basic methods to manipulate data, but when doing complex operations, ArrayCollection offers methods that could take several operations to accomplish using a normal array.

Accessing external data

There are a few ways to access or load external data and assets in Flex. Bringing content dynamically into our applications is essential in order to create content that intelligently loads assets on demand, to adapt to the audience by displaying localized interfaces, or simply to better organize large applications into more manageable pieces.

As part of this process, we are going to take a closer look at one of the classes we used the most in our exercises: the HTTPService.

HTTPService is used to get data from a server by making an HTTP (Hypertext Protocol) request to a specific URL and obtaining a response from a server. You can also optionally pass parameters to the URL.

In simple terms, a request is sent to a server via a URL; the server awaits the request and, based on the URL given, returns data back to the client. When exchanging data with a server, Flex is extremely versatile and compliant with almost every standard protocol out there.

The HTTPService tag is a neat way to make an HTTP request. As shown in Figure 7-14, we open the HTTPService tag and give it a unique ID so we can reference it later. Then we have a url property in which we enter the location of the file we need—in this case, the myXMLFile.xml file. As you can see, this can be a full URL or a local file as long as the SWF resides in the same directory as the file we are requesting. The resultFormat allows us to indicate how we want to deserialize the file we get back from the server—in other words, whether we want to treat it as an object, array, XML, FlashVar, text, or ECMAScript for XML (E4X). For this example, we chose E4X; you will see why in a moment.

```
<mx:Application xmlns:mx="http://www.adobe.com/2006/mxml"
    layout="absolute" creationComplete="myData.send()">
    <mx:HTTPService id="myData" url="myXML.xml" resultFormat="e4x"/>
```

Figure 7-14. HTTPService

Finally, the HTTPService executes the request as soon as we call its send() method. In this example, we call this method at the application's creationComplete event.

E4X

In essence, ECMAScript for XML (E4X) introduces a convenient way of manipulating and extracting data for XML with simple regular expressions and dot notation.

Figure 7-15 shows a simple XML file called bookstore.xml.

```
<bookstore>
    <book>
        <title>Foundation Flex for Designers</title>
        <author>Greg Goralski & LordAlex Leon</author>
    </book>
</bookstore>
```

Figure 7-15. Simple XML file

Once the XML file is loaded, you can easily access data using ActionScript notation. For example, bookstore.book.title would give you Foundation Flex for Designers. Figure 7-16 shows a working example that can be used to create more elaborate projects.

```
<?xml version="1.0" encoding="utf-8"?>
<mx:Application xmlns:mx="http://www.adobe.com/2006/mxml"
    layout="absolute" creationComplete="bookstore.send()">
    <mx:Script>
        <![CDATA[
        //Import statements
        import mx.rpc.events.ResultEvent;
        private function onResult( event:ResultEvent ):void
        {
                var bookstore:XML = event.result as XML;
                trace(bookstore.book.title);
                // output is Foundation Flex for Designers
        }
        ]]>
    </mx:Script>
    <mx:HTTPService id="bookstore" url="bookstore.xml"
        resultFormat="e4x" result = "onResult(event);" />
</mx:Application>
```

Figure 7-16. Working E4X example

Accessing data in this way makes working with XML much simpler and can be used to manage complex data. This example only scratches the tip of iceberg but illustrates the purpose of E4X.

SWFLoader

SWFLoader is used to load and display other SWF files into Flex. It allows you to scale the content you are loading, as well as monitor the loading progress (Figure 7-17).

145

In Figure 7-17 we use @Embed, which tells Flex to embed the asset at compile time, meaning the image is bundled along with the final SWF. However, you may choose not use @Embed, and the compiler will load the asset at runtime instead.

The Height and Width parameters allow you to set dimensions for the file being loaded.

```
<mx:SWFLoader id="LoadExternal source"
              source="@Embed(source='externalSWF.swf')"
              height="350"
              width="350"/>
```

Figure 7-17. SWFLoader

ActionScript and MXML

The most common and easiest way to add ActionScript to a Flex application via MXML is to type it in the Source view of the MXML Editor. Place the ActionScript after the opening tags and before the component tags. To separate the ActionScript from the MXML components, place the ActionScript within <mx:Script> tags (Figure 7-18).

```
    Source      Design
 1  <?xml version="1.0" encoding="utf-8"?>
 2  <mx:Application xmlns:mx="http://www.adobe.com/2006/mxml" layout="absolute">
 3  <mx:Script>
 4      <![CDATA[
 5
 6
 7      ]]>
 8  </mx:Script>
 9  </mx:Application>
10
```

Figure 7-18. Placing ActionScript in Flex

This approach requires less direct typing of code than it appears to at first glance. By entering the start of a tag for you, Flex attempts to give you the options that begin with what you are typing. So typing <mx:S will give you the Script tag (Figure 7-19).

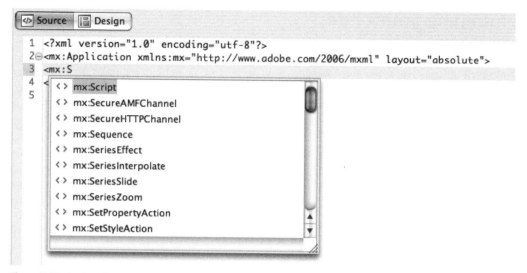

Figure 7-19. Options for an MXML tag provided while typing

Close the tag by typing >, as shown in Figure 7-20, and press Enter. Notice in Figure 7-20 that some extra code has been added automatically.

This piece of code creates a character data section. In this section, everything you type will not be part of an MXML tag. This is where we place our ActionScript code.

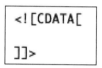

Figure 7-20. Character data section

Importing ActionScript classes into Flex

Another thing worth noting is that it is easy just to add a .* to the end of a package path, but this throws up a few issues. First, other developers may not know exactly which class you have imported from that package if the code is particularly complex or abstract. Second, the compiler will go through every class in that package and check to see if it was used, which slows down the compiler. Although the slowdown is not an issue on a small project, it can be tiresome on large builds.

Often the first pieces of code that are added are the `import` statements. The `import` statements indicate to the compiler that you are going to declare an instance of the class you have imported. For example, in Chapter 12 we create a media center that works with videos, using the class VideoPlayer. In this case, the statement looks like Figure 7-21.

```
import mx.controls.videoClasses.VideoPlayer
```

Figure 7-21. The import statement

Maintaining your code

Comments are pieces of text that are added to the code to help a person looking at the code to make more sense of it faster. These are extra statements that the computer ignores but that help us understand what is happening in the code. These comments are ways of communicating to the people that may be reading the code. They allow the person who created the code to explain it, mentioning bugs or kludged pieces of code along the way. This becomes especially important when developing in a team or if you return to the code after a period of time. As an extra bonus, comments can be used to generate documentation. A program called ASDoc (included in the Flex SDK) can read specific markers in comment blocks and convert them to HTML files.

Figure 7-22 shows two ways of putting comments into code. There is no difference between the two forms of commenting except that one is easier for single lines and the other is better for larger pieces of text.

```
/*
This text gets ignored by the computer,
but it can help you learn or remember what a
certain part of the code is supposed to be doing
*/

//    Another way to add comments.
```

Figure 7-22. Two ways of adding comments

Controlling flow with events

Both ActionScript 3.0 and Flex are based on an event model. By that, we mean that all interaction, method invocation, and so forth are generally handled by associating a specific event with it. Methods contain the specific pieces of functionality that need to be executed, and events trigger those pieces of functionality.

Every component has a series of events that are associated with it. You can also create custom events. You can find the events for a component in the Category view of its properties. Figure 7-23 shows some of the events that are available for a button.

You can see that there are a lot of possible events. Essentially anything that can happen to a button—creating, dragging, rolling over—can trigger a method. The most common events are click and creationComplete. To trigger a method on any of these events, you add the name of the method next to the event name. In Figure 7-24, you can see that click is calling a method called close. The event in the parentheses is the instance of the Event class that can be used by the method that is called.

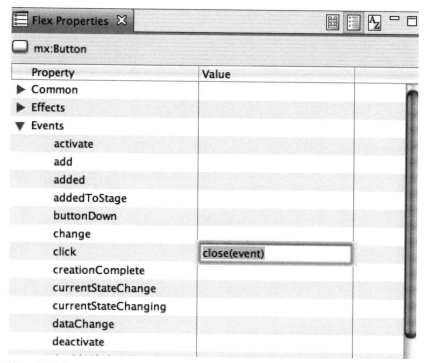

Figure 7-23. Events properties for the Button component in Category view

The changes made in the component properties are reflected in the MXML for the button, as shown in Figure 7-24.

```
<mx:Button id="myCloseButton" click="close(event)" />
```

Figure 7-24. Button event in MXML

Events can be triggered in the MXML or in ActionScript. Figure 7-25 shows the ActionScript equivalent of the MXML button event.

```
myCloseButton.addEventListener(Event.CLICK, close());
```

Figure 7-25. Button event in ActionScript

You'll notice that the ActionScript version doesn't declare the event object that will be passed to the handler. This is because the Event Listener in ActionScript 3.0 is aware of the event. So if we had not included a parameter in our close() method's signature of type Event, when someone clicked our button it would throw an error. An event can trigger more than one method.

Binding data

Most applications will rely on one form of data or another. This may take the form of a list of names of images, or the options in a combo box. In Flex one of them is the dataProvider.

In Flex, a data structure that contains data required by a component or control is referred to as a dataProvider. Many Flex components have a property called DataProvider. This property generally takes in some form of complex data, such as an array. For example, say we wanted to use an array to populate a combo box. We could set that array to be the dataProvider for our ComboBox. Figure 7-26 shows how this would look in the Source view. Note that the name of the dataProvider is placed in curly brackets in the dataProvider field.

```
<mx:Script>
    <![CDATA[

    [Bindable]
    public var myPictures:Array = ["Landscape.jpg", "Portrait.jpg", "Macro.jpg"];
    ]]>
</mx:Script>

<mx:ComboBox id="Pictures" dataProvider="{myPictures}"/>
```

Figure 7-26. ComboBox with an array as a dataProvider

We use the curly brackets to tell Flex we want to bind a certain value to a component control. In our example, we are binding the array myPictures to the ComboBox. Once the binding is created, if we dynamically change the value of one of the pictures in the array, the ComboBox will be immediately updated as well. This is the magic of data binding.

The last ingredient involved in binding a variable to a component is the keyword [Bindable]. We place it above the value we want to bind; otherwise the binding will not work.

You can also connect the ComboBox to a dataProvider in the Design view by setting the component's properties (Figure 7-27).

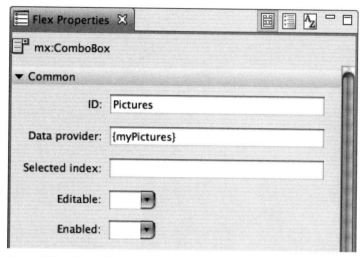

Figure 7-27. Adding a dataProvider using Component properties

Summary

In Flex, you have a combination of ActionScript and MXML tags to create the ability of your project to interact with the user. Although as a designer you will not likely create the ActionScript yourself, it is important to see how the code connects with your components.

The methods that are created in ActionScript are called on by the events of the components to take an action. Data is often used to populate components through the dataProvider property.

This has been a quick overview of coding concepts. To delve deeper into this topic, check out *Foundation ActionScript 3.0 with Flash CS3 and Flex* by Sean McSharry, Steve Webster, and Todd Yard (friends of ED, 2007). In the next chapter, we will use some of these coding techniques to create an XML-driven photo gallery.

Chapter 8

FLEX PHOTO GALLERY

What we'll cover in this chapter:

- Repeaters
- XML within Flex
- Animation

Files used in this chapter:

- assets folder
- PhotoGallery-Complete.zip

In this chapter, we'll look at bringing together some of what you've already learned, combining it with some new visual effects, and creating an XML-driven photo gallery. Let's start by seeing what it will look like in the end (see Figure 8-1); load the complete photo gallery from the code download for this book at www.friendsofed.com. Select File ➤ Import ➤ Existing Projects into Workspace. In the resulting dialog box, click the radio button Select the Archive File and browse to select PhotoGallery-Complete.zip. Click Finish. This will bring the entire project, complete with assets, MXML, and styling, into Flex Builder.

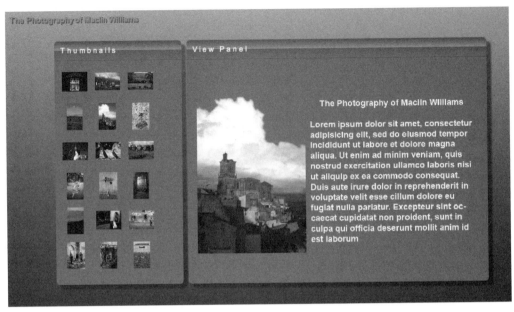

Figure 8-1. Our final picture gallery

The images that we're using for this example are from a wonderful Toronto-based photographer named Maclin Williams.

Starting off

Let's begin by examining the files provided at the book's website for this chapter. The assets folder is critical for this example because it contains both the images as well as the XML file that helps us load them. In the folder called assets you will find a folder called pictures that holds 18 JPEG images. As Figure 8-2 shows, they are named 1.jpg through 18.jpg and are the images that populate our gallery.

The second important file in the assets folder is pictures.xml (Figure 8-3).

This simple XML file lists the names and location of each of the pictures that we want to use. It is possible to have this information in the MXML file, but by using an external XML we are allowing the images to be updated without opening the original Flex application. A photographer, for example, can easily open an XML file and change which images she would like displayed. A photographer would be less comfortable opening the entire Flex application to make such a change.

1. Create a new Flex project named PhotoGallery by selecting File ➤ New ➤ Flex Project and completing the default dialog boxes.

   With the project created, we'll link the assets folder to the project.

2. Save the assets folder to a location on your computer (My Documents on a PC or Documents on a Mac works fine).

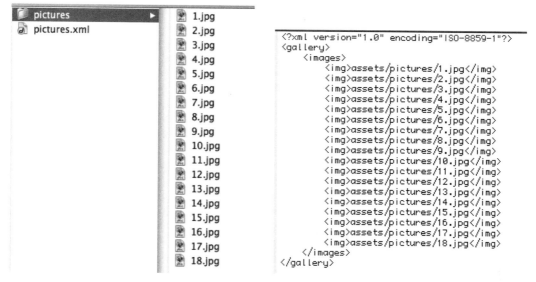

Figure 8-2. The contents of the assets folder

Figure 8-3. The XML file holds image names.

3. Create a new folder by selecting File ➤ New ➤ Folder (Figure 8-4).

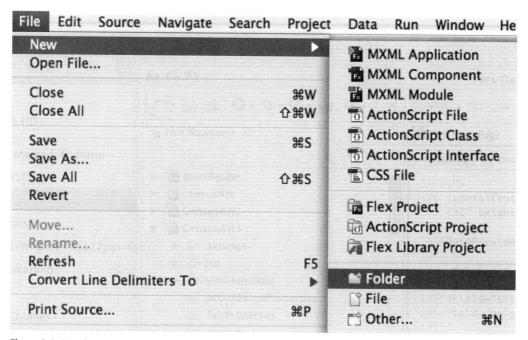

Figure 8-4. Creating a new folder

4. In the New Folder dialog box (see Figure 8-5), click Advanced. In the panel that opens at the bottom of the dialog box, click the Link to folder in the file system option and browse to the location of the assets folder.

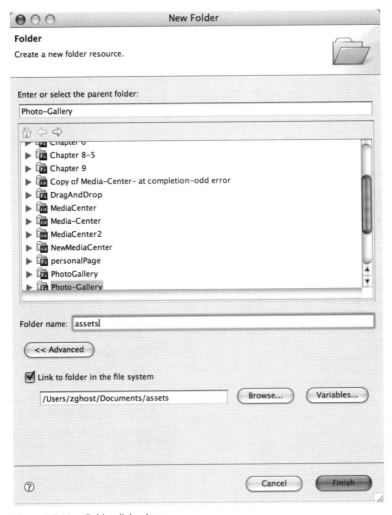

Figure 8-5. New Folder dialog box

Notice that now the assets folder is a *linked* folder with this project. This means that the folder has not been copied into the project but that the files are accessible to it (Figure 8-6). This would be useful if you wanted to share assets across projects.

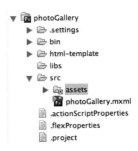

Figure 8-6. Automatically created folder location

Building the Thumbnails panel

The first of the two panels that make up the gallery is the Thumbnails panel. This panel contains the small version of each image. The final result will look something like Figure 8-7.

Figure 8-7. The Thumbnails panel

1. Begin by placing a Panel component, from the Layout folder, into the Design view of your Flex project. Give this panel the ID of thumbsPanel so that we can identify it in the MXML code. Also, give it the Title of Thumbnails to reinforce for the user what this panel contains (Figure 8-8).

2. Since this panel is to hold three columns and six rows of thumbnails, we should give it a size of about 250 pixels wide and 460 pixels tall. This gives us enough room to lay out all the images and have some space between them for a scaling effect that we'll be creating later in this chapter. Since we want this panel to stay roughly in the middle of the screen regardless of the resolution size, let's give it an absolute location based on the center of the screen. You specify this by setting both the top and side layout handles to center. The distance from the center of the application is defined by the layout constraints that appear when you set the layout handles to center, as shown in Figure 8-9. Set the Horizontal Center to –325 and the Vertical Center to –95.

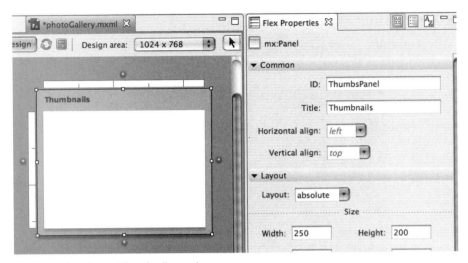

Figure 8-8. Creating our Thumbnails panel

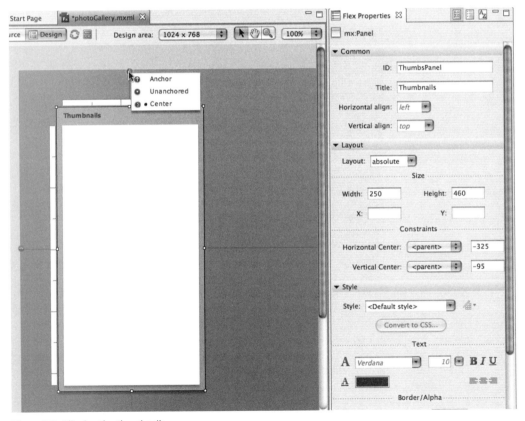

Figure 8-9. Aligning the thumbnails

The Tile component

As we create this panel, we'll attempt to reduce repetition for a couple of reasons. One is to avoid repetitive work, and the other is to include scalability. Instead of creating 18 different thumbnail pictures and laying them out manually, we'll create one and use the tools in Flex Builder to lay out and repeat the Image component.

The first of these tools is the Tile component. This component is useful for laying out a set of like objects, such as a set of products. The Tile component responds to the amount of space it is given to organize the set of images that we are going to send to it.

1. Place a Tile component inside the Panel component. You will be presented with a dialog box that lets you set the size of the Tile component. Click OK, and stretch the Tile component until it fills up the entire content area of the Panel component (Figure 8-10).

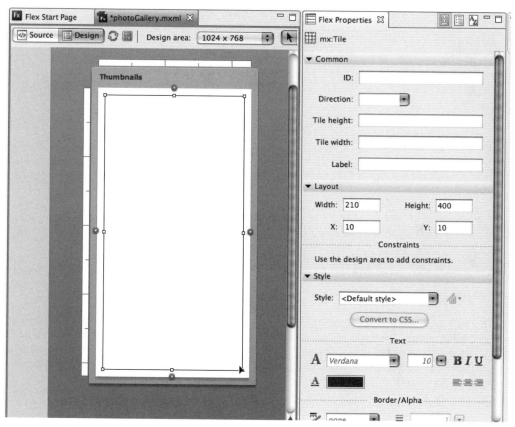

Figure 8-10. Tile component

2. In the Tile component, place one HBox component, and then place an Image component inside that. The HBox component will be a bit larger than the image, which will give it space for the zooming effect later, and will help us properly center the image. This HBox should be about 70 by 70 pixels (Figure 8-11), so type 70 into both boxes in the Insert HBox window.

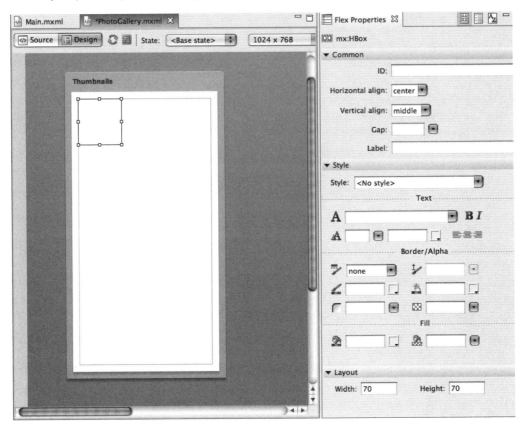

Figure 8-11. HBox component

3. The Image component should be 50 pixels by 50 pixels. This size is large enough to get a sense of the photograph but still leaves enough space for all the images. The Image component should sit at the top left within the HBox (Figure 8-12). Change this to be centered by setting the Horizontal and Vertical alignment pulldowns within the HBox component to center and middle, respectively.

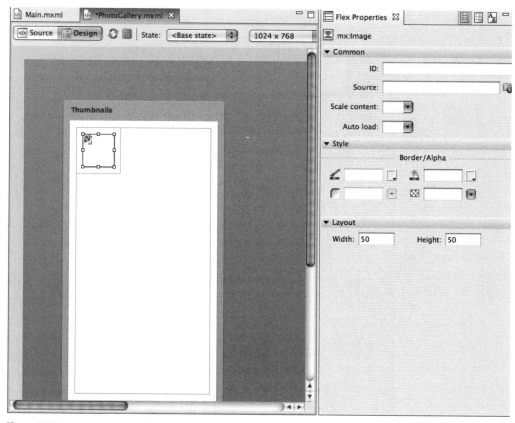

Figure 8-12. Image component in position

Proper alignment

If you look closely at the Image component, even without an image present, you can see how the images will ultimately be aligned. Figure 8-13 shows that the icon for the missing picture is aligned to the top and left.

Figure 8-13. Image component
with corner alignment

If we leave the component with this default setting, our thumbnails will look a bit odd as some are landscape and some are portrait. Figure 8-14 shows how the thumbnails would look in this setting.

Figure 8-14. Thumbnails panel with top-right image alignment

This alignment, though not tragic, is distinctly odd. In order to change this, we need to modify the settings for the component. The standard properties for an Image component give us very little to go on (see Figure 8-15). There are no properties that affect the alignment. For this reason, we need to dig deeper into the component.

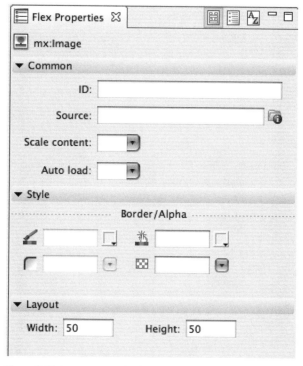

Figure 8-15. Image properties in Standard view

Looking along the top of the Properties panel, you'll see a set of icons. These icons allow us to change how we look at the component (Figure 8-16).

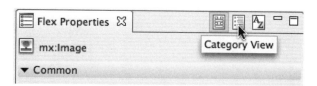

Figure 8-16. Switching to Category view

So far we have been using the Standard view, which shows us the most commonly used properties. The next view is the Category view, which gives us access to many more properties but can be a bit overwhelming at first (Figure 8-17).

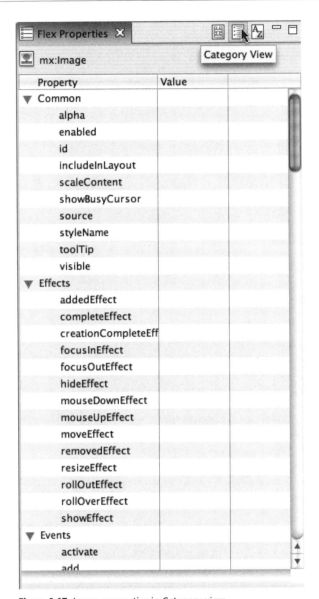

Figure 8-17. Image properties in Category view

Close to the bottom of this list, in the Styles category, you will find the settings to align the image. To change the values of the attributes in the Category view, click in the Values column next to horizontalAlign and verticalAlign. A pulldown box will appear with the alignment options. Select center for horizontalAlign and middle for verticalAlign (Figure 8-18).

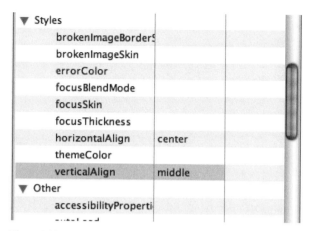

Figure 8-18. Center alignment of Image component

Looking at the Image component now, you can see that regardless the shape of the image, it will now be held in the middle (Figure 8-19).

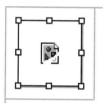

Figure 8-19. Image component with center alignment

Bringing in the XML

Bringing an XML file into Flex is quite simple, but it does need to be done directly in the Source view:

1. First create an HTTPService that brings the data into the application. Switch to the Source view, and add the following code directly underneath the opening <Application> tag: `<mx:HTTPService id="galleryData" url="assets/pictures.xml"/>`. This code tells the service where to find the XML, and gives the service a name, galleryData, that we can use later. The pictures.xml file is in the assets folder that we brought into this project.

2. Define when this service will be called; you can associate it with a button or an event. In this case, because we want the XML to load right when the application is created, add the following code directly to the end of the opening <Application> tag: `creationComplete="galleryData.send()"`.

Your new MXML should look like Figure 8-20.

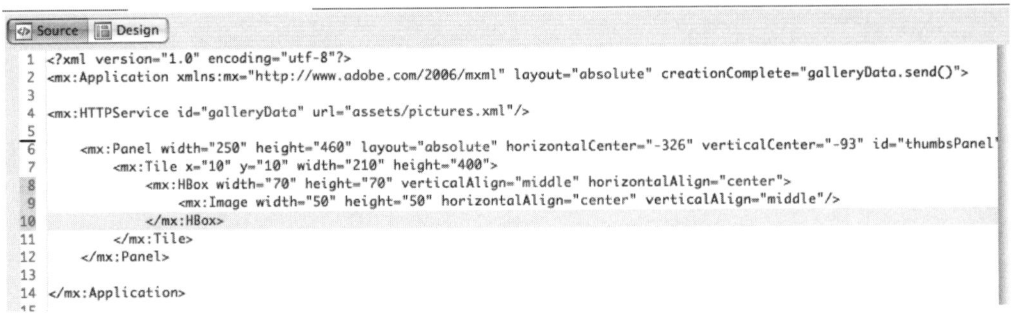

Figure 8-20. MXML with HTTPService

The data in the XML file now gets placed into the dataProvider called galleryData when we run the project. We'll use this dataProvider to populate our thumbnails. This is done through a repeater, which we discuss in the next section.

Getting the computer to do the work: repeaters

A repeater is a piece of code that allows you to do a similar step many times. In this case, the similar step is the creation of a thumbnail image, and placing an image from our XML into it. For those with programming experience, this is a form of the for loop.

In this example, we want to repeat the image and the HBox that helps us format it. So we put a repeater tag around these two objects in the Source view. The tag looks like this;

```
<mx:Repeater dataProvider="{galleryData.lastResult.gallery.images.img}" ➥
id="imageRepeater">
<mx:HBox width="70" height="70" verticalAlign="middle" ➥
horizontalAlign="center">
<mx:Image width="50" height="50" horizontalAlign="center" ➥
verticalAlign="middle"/>
</mx:HBox>
</mx:Repeater>
```

Note that the first part of the tag goes before the code that you want to repeat, the HBox in our case, and the closing tag goes after it. The dataProvider is set up based on the structure of our XML file. This setup pulls in the data and keeps repeating until it hits the end of the XML.

By adding this tag to your MXML, you should end up with something that looks like Figure 8-21.

```
?xml version="1.0" encoding="utf-8"?>
<mx:Application xmlns:mx="http://www.adobe.com/2006/mxml" layout="absolute" creationComplete="galleryData.send()">

<mx:HTTPService id="galleryData" url="assets/pictures.xml"/>

    <mx:Panel width="272" height="460" layout="absolute" horizontalCenter="-346" verticalCenter="-7"
        id="thumbsPanel" title="Thumbnails">
        <mx:Tile x="10" y="10" width="242" height="400">
        <mx:Repeater dataProvider="{galleryData.lastResult.gallery.images.img}" id="imageRepeater">
            <mx:HBox width="70" height="70" verticalAlign="middle" horizontalAlign="center" id="viewerPanel">
                <mx:Image width="50" height="50" horizontalAlign="center" verticalAlign="middle"
                    source="{imageRepeater.currentItem}" click="getImage(event)"/>
            </mx:HBox>
        </mx:Repeater>
        </mx:Tile>
    </mx:Panel>

</mx:Application>
```

Figure 8-21. MXML with a repeater

We use the repeater to create each thumbnail image. As each thumbnail is created, the latest image is added to it. This can be done in either the Design or Source view, but we'll show it in the Design view so that it is more visual.

1. Switch back to the Design view, and select the Image component. If you are in the Category view, you will see a variety of component properties. The most important of these is the Source property, under the Common heading at the top. This property defines which image will be placed into the component.

2. Type {imageRepeater.currentItem} into the Source for the Image component.

3. Test how your Thumbnails panel looks like by choosing Run ➤ Run PhotoGallery. Your panel should look like Figure 8-22.

You may want to tinker with the size of the panel to get the right effect. Notice that as soon as a Tile component runs out of space to show the images, it creates a scrollbar to allow the user to see the entire set of images. Also notice that we never told the repeater exactly how many images there are. It took this information on its own from the number of entries in the XML file. This means that if we want to add an image, we can just add the entry to the XML. No MXML needs to be changed. This makes updating a breeze.

Figure 8-22. Thumbnails panel showing the scrollbar

167

Creating the View panel

When a user clicks a thumbnail image, we want a larger version of that image to appear in a panel next to the Thumbnails panel. Let's call this panel View Panel and place it to the right of the first panel we created.

1. Drag a new panel to the right of the original panel. We want this panel to be the same height as the first panel, but we'll make it wider as it will hold a large version of the image. A good width for this panel is 580 pixels and the height is 460 pixels. Add an ID of viewerPanel and a Title of View Panel, as shown in Figure 8-23.

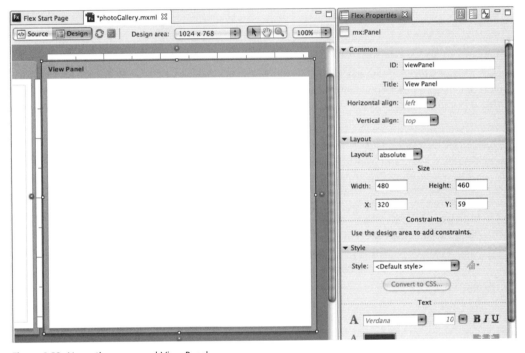

Figure 8-23. Name the new panel View Panel.

2. Give this panel a similar layout to the first panel, with an absolute layout anchored to the center (Figure 8-24).

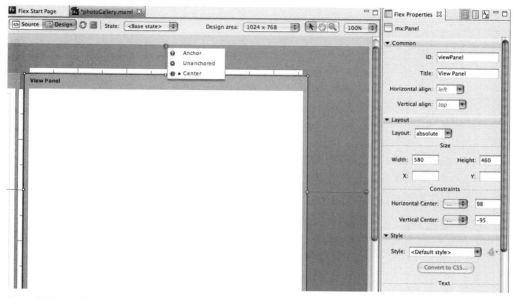

Figure 8-24. Use these layout settings to align our panel.

3. In the panel, place an Image component and stretch it out to take up most of the content area of the panel.

4. Give this Image component an ID of previewImg.

We will create some code that displays the same image that's on the thumbnail the user presses, but right now the image is empty. To avoid having a blank area in our design, we'll include an image location directly in the Source property of the Image component (Figure 8-25).

5. Click the browse icon to the right of the Source field and find the image firstImage.png in the assets folder.

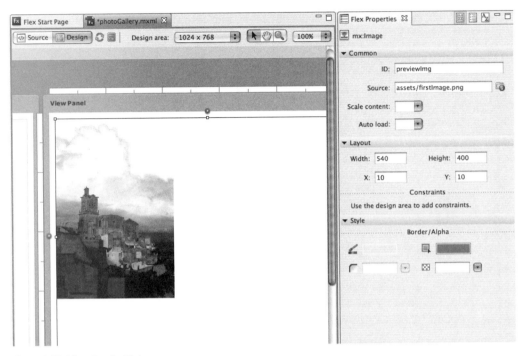

Figure 8-25. View Panel with image

Connecting the Thumbnails and View panels

We need a small piece of ActionScript to send the image from the Thumbnails panel to the View Panel. You can find this piece of code in the file code.txt in the code download for this book at www. friendsofed.com. You can copy this code directly below the HTTPService in your MXML (Figure 8-26).

```
 6    <mx:Script>
 7        <![CDATA[
 8            import mx.events.*;
 9            private function getImage(event:Event):void
10            {
11                previewImg.load(event.currentTarget.getRepeaterItem());
12            }
13        ]]>
14    </mx:Script>
```

Figure 8-26. ActionScript connecting Thumbnails to View Panel

This code pulls from the repeater to get the correct image. Now that we have created this function, we need to call it when the thumbnail is clicked. Do this in the Design view, in the component properties.

1. Select the thumbnail Image component. Notice that there are a limited number of properties that can be adjusted in the Standard view (Figure 8-27).

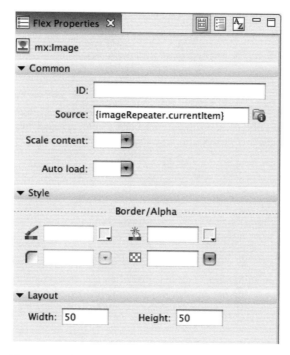

Figure 8-27. Thumbnail image properties

2. As we did earlier in this chapter, switch to the Category view of the component properties to get access to more properties, especially for events and effects. Here we can call any function to run based on an action. In this case, when the user clicks the thumbnail, we want the function that we just created to run (in this case, getImage(event)). So we type getImage(event) in the Value column of the click event, as shown in Figure 8-28.

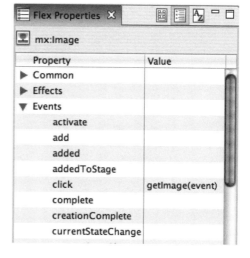

Figure 8-28 . Type getImage(event) in the Value column.

Run the project to see the interaction.

Adding some sizzle

To make the interface more responsive, you often want to create a feedback animation to reinforce for the user what is selected. In our case, if you go back to the original example, we have our thumbnails grow and glow on rollover.

To create an animation within Flex, we first build it in the MXML, then attach it to an event, such as a rollover.

1. Let's start by creating the effect of the rollover animation. In the Source view, add a `<Parallel>` tag. This tag is used when you want more than one visual change to happen at once, as we will. It also allows us to use one name for a set of actions. In our case, we will call it over since we will be using it for a rollover (Figure 8-29). Type this code after the ActionScript in the Source view.

```
<mx:Parallel id="over">


</mx:Parallel>
```

Figure 8-29. Type this code inside the opening
`<Parallel>` tag.

2. The first part of the effect is a zoom. Between the `<Parallel>` tags, create a new tag that defines the kind of animation (e.g., a zoom), the duration in milliseconds, and any other needed attributes (e.g., the extent of zoom), as shown in Figure 8-30. As you can see, the zoom lasts 100 milliseconds and scales to 1.4 times (or 140%) of the original size.

```
<mx:Parallel id="over">
    <mx:Zoom  duration="100" zoomHeightTo="1.4" zoomWidthTo="1.4"/>
</mx:Parallel>
```

Figure 8-30. Create a new tag that defines the kind of animation.

3. Adding the glow effect is similar, except that it has more attributes. Add the code shown in Figure 8-31 to your `<Parallel>` tag.

```
<mx:Parallel id="over">
    <mx:Zoom  duration="100" zoomHeightTo="1.4" zoomWidthTo="1.4"/>
    <mx:Glow id="glowImage" duration="300"
    alphaFrom="1.0" alphaTo="0.3"
    blurXFrom="0.0" blurXTo="30.0"
    blurYFrom="0.0" blurYTo="30.0"
    color="0xFFFFFF"/>
</mx:Parallel>
```

Figure 8-31. Adding the glow effect

4. Now we've defined what happens when a user rolls over a thumbnail, we need to define what happens when they roll off it. For the rollout actions, create a new <Parallel> tag and follow the same steps but reverse the values. For example, instead of scaling to 1.4 times the normal size, scale back to 1 times the normal size (Figure 8-32).

```
<mx:Parallel id="out">
    <mx:Zoom  duration="100" zoomHeightTo="1" zoomWidthTo="1" />
    <mx:Glow id="unglowImage" duration="200"
    alphaFrom="0.3" alphaTo="1.0"
    blurXFrom="30.0" blurXTo="0.0"
    blurYFrom="30.0" blurYTo="0.0"
    color="0xFFFFFF"/>
</mx:Parallel>
```

Figure 8-32. Defining the rollout actions

5. Return to the Design view and select the thumbnail Image component. In the properties in the Category view, type {out} for the rollOutEffect and {over} for the rollOverEffect. This will connect the actions to the thumbnail images. Since we are using a repeater to create all the thumbnail images except the first, these effects will be added to all the images (Figure 8-33).

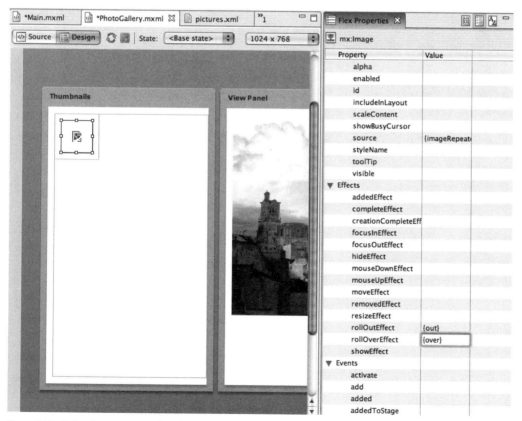

Figure 8-33. Animations connected to thumbnail images

Finishing touches

Now that we have connected the animations and the thumbnails shown in the View Panel, the functionality of the photo gallery is complete. To make this gallery the same as the original design that you saw at the start of this chapter, all we need to do is add some CSS styling (see Chapter 2). Figure 8-34 shows the design before CSS styling.

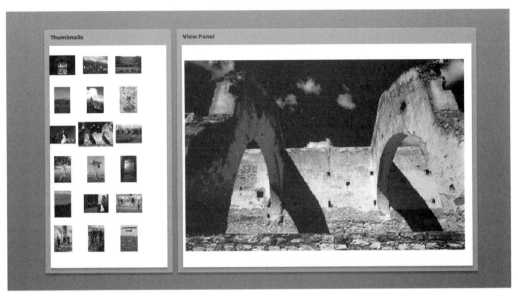

Figure 8-34. Design before CSS styling

The styling we'll use is included with the download files for this chapter in the file PhotoGallery.css. We've added the name of the photographer along the top by using a couple of label components. Figure 8-35 shows the final design.

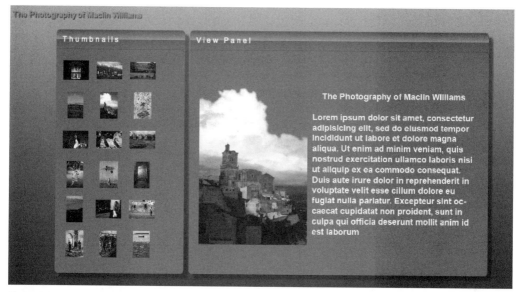

Figure 8-35. Our final design

Summary

While creating our photo gallery, we took advantage of some significant new components and techniques. We used the Tile component to create our Thumbnails panel and used a repeater to populate the thumbnails. We aligned our images via the alignment properties on both the image and the HBox that held them.

We also explored how to create animation effects. In our example we used the glow and zoom animations to create the rollover effects for our thumbnails.

In the next chapter, we'll use a similar basic design layout with more advanced functionality. Specifically, we'll begin working with video clips instead of static images, and we'll explore drag-and-drop functionality.

Chapter 9

FLEX VIDEO GALLERY WITH DRAG-AND-DROP

What we'll cover in this chapter:

- Drag-and-drop List controls
- Manually adding drag-and-drop
- Working with videos

Files used in this chapter:

- Assets folder
- dragAndDropCode.txt

In the previous chapter, you learned how to create a photo gallery that pulls images in through XML. Next we are going to build off this design and take it to the next level. We'll work with video instead of stills. Also, instead of using a button click to select a video, we'll use the drag-and-drop capabilities that are built into Flex.

Using drag-and-drop is a great way to give your interface a more tactile feel, and it allows for greater complexity within the interface by allowing the user to drag an object to multiple locations.

Drag-and-drop in Flex

The Flex development platform includes the Drag and Drop Manager, which allows you to select a component, drag it over the top of another component, and add it to that component. All Flex components support drag-and-drop, but some have extra support to make it easier. These are components such as Lists and DataGrids. We'll start by creating a simple example using components that have this extra support, and then follow up with a more elaborate example. The second example will involve putting drag-and-drop functionality into a photo gallery using a manual method, which is pretty complex but gives you greater control over the interaction.

There are three stages to a drag-and-drop operation:

- The initiation, when the user first selects a component and, while holding down the mouse button, moves that component.

- The dragging, when the component is being moved. During this time an image called the *drag proxy* is displayed that represents the selected component. We can control this proxy image to get various effects. The original component is referred to as the *drag source*.

- The dropping. When the dragged component is put over the top of another component, that component becomes a drop target. Flex analyzes whether the data of the dragged component can go into the drop target. If it can, then you can release the dragged component and it enters the drop target. If it cannot, then the dragged component returns to its original position.

Drag-and-drop with List controls

Some components make drag-and-drop very easy because it is built into those components. Examples of the components that work this way include the List, DataGrid, Tile List, and Tree controls. We'll create an example of this kind of built-in drag-and-drop first.

1. Create a new Flex application (Figure 9-1).

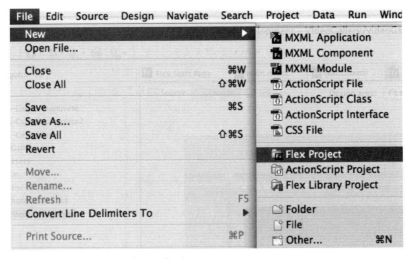

Figure 9-1. Creating a new Flex application

2. Name the project DragAndDrop (Figure 9-2). Click Next and then Finish.

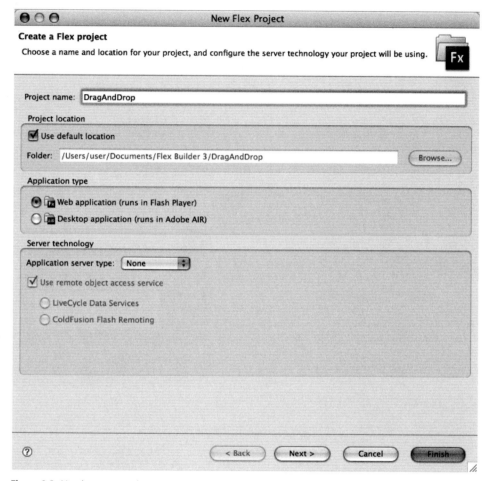

Figure 9-2. Naming your project

3. In this project we'll passing data across three different lists. In the Design view, start by placing one list component onto the stage (Figure 9-3).

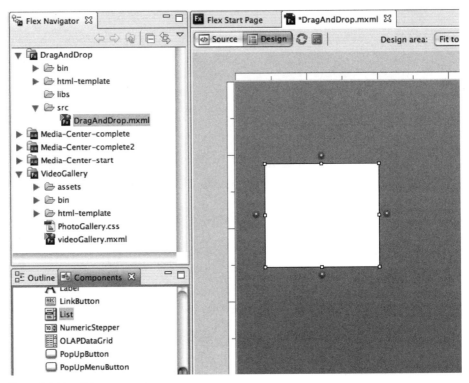

Figure 9-3. New List component

This component will serve as our template for the future ones.

4. As you saw in Chapter 8, components have many more editable properties than are presented in the Standard view of the Properties panel. The ones that apply to drag-and-drop are examples of the properties that are not visible in the Standard view. Select Category View to access these properties (Figure 9-4).

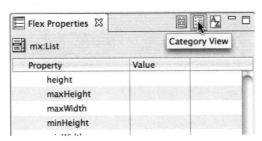

Figure 9-4. Switching to the Category view

5. The properties that we will be working with—dragEnabled, dragMoveEnabled, and dropEnabled— are in the category Other. dragEnabled means that you can drag items from this list, dragMoveEnabled means items can be moved around in this list by dragging, and dropEnabled means that items can be placed into this component. Set all three to true so that we have the most flexibility within this interaction (Figure 9-5).

6. Adjust the size of the component so that it is 150 by 150 pixels. Without this step, the component will readjust to the size of the data that is provided.

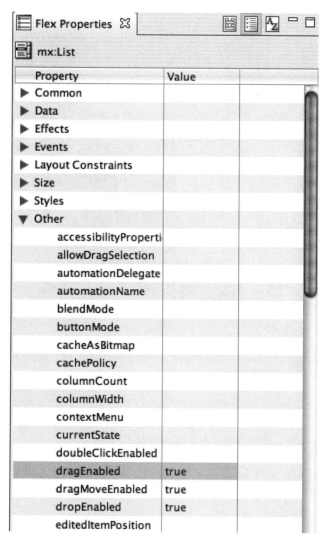

Figure 9-5. Enabling drag in the List properties

7. Now that we have one component that has been made useful for drag-and-drop, copy this component twice to create three identical lists (Figure 9-6). Following best practice, give each component a unique ID, such as List1, List2, and List3.

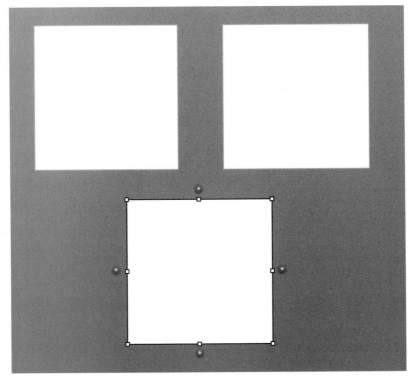

Figure 9-6. Duplicated List components

8. In order to add some data to drag between the lists, select the dataProvider property of the first list. This dataProvider can be applied to any of the List components. You'll find it in the Data section of the Category view and also in the properties in the Standard view. In the Value field for this property, enter a list of items, enclosed in square brackets and separated by commas (Figure 9-7).

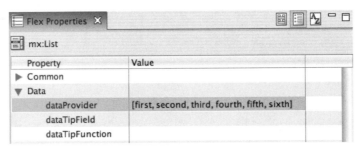

Figure 9-7. Adding data to the List component

9. Run the application to see how the drag-and-drop works. Notice that in this example, we can move the text from any list around multiple times and have control over where in the list our dropped text goes (Figure 9-8).

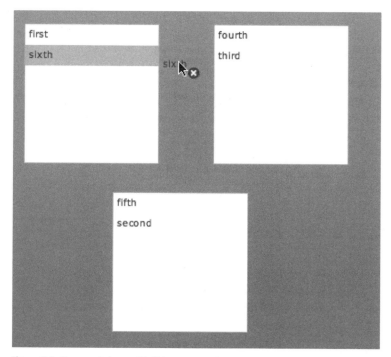

Figure 9-8. Drag-and-drop with List components

Also notice that Flex lets you know when you are over an area that is not a suitable drop area by displaying a red x icon.

Manually adding drag-and-drop support

Instead of starting from scratch for the next example, let's use what we have already built. Since this application is going to be very similar in layout to the photo gallery from Chapter 8, let's create a copy of that project to work from.

1. To create a copy of a project, right-click on the existing project (Control-click on a Mac) and select Copy (Figure 9-9).

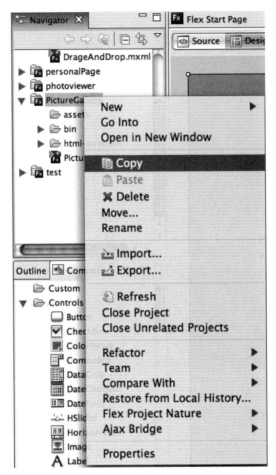

Figure 9-9. Copying an existing application

2. Right/Control-click again and select Paste. You will be given the option to rename the project and change its location (Figure 9-10). Rename it VideoGallery. This renames the folder for the application but not the name of the default MXML file.

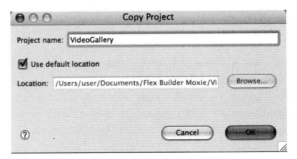

Figure 9-10. Renaming the application

3. To change the MXML file name, right/Control-click on the existing file name and select Rename. Rename the file VideoGallery (Figure 9-11).

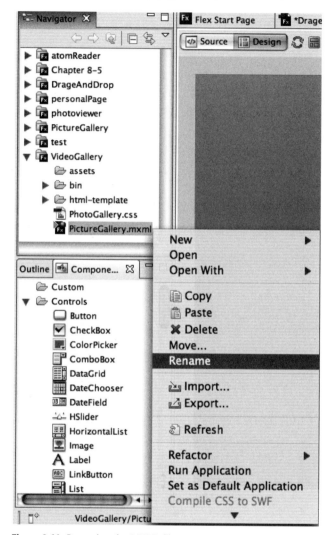

Figure 9-11. Renaming the MXML file

We can leave the CSS file named as it is to keep things simpler.

4. Next we want to replace the assets in this folder with the assets that are provided for this chapter in the code download for this book at www.friendsofed.com. The assets folder contains the videos and the XML file that controls them. As you can see in Figure 9-12, it is structured very much like the assets folder that we used in Chapter 8.

Figure 9-12. The assets file structure

The XML file is also structured the same way that the Chapter 8 XML was structured (Figure 9-13).

```
<?xml version="1.0" encoding="ISO-8859-1"?>
<gallery>
    <videos>
        <video>assets/videos/video1.flv</video>
        <video>assets/videos/video2.flv</video>
        <video>assets/videos/video3.flv</video>
        <video>assets/videos/video4.flv</video>
        <video>assets/videos/video5.flv</video>
        <video>assets/videos/video6.flv</video>
        <video>assets/videos/video7.flv</video>
        <video>assets/videos/video8.flv</video>
        <video>assets/videos/video9.flv</video>
    </videos>
</gallery>
```

Figure 9-13. Videos XML file

5. Copy the assets folder from the code download directly over the assets folder in the video gallery. This will overwrite the existing files and replace them with the new ones.

6. We will be doing quite a bit of editing of the MXML file and this is easiest in the Source view. Switch to the Source view for the VideoGallery project. Since the name of the XML file has changed, we will have to change the name of the XML file that is called by the HTTPService.

The new HTTPService will look like Figure 9-14.

```
</> Source    Design
 1  <?xml version="1.0" encoding="utf-8"?>
 2  <mx:Application xmlns:mx="http://www.adobe.com/2006/mxml" layout="c
 3
 4  <mx:HTTPService id="galleryData" url="assets/videos.xml"/>
 5
```

Figure 9-14. Changed HTTPService

7. We also need to change the XML at the point where we bring the values from the file into the repeater. This is at the dataProvider. The existing dataProvider looks like Figure 9-15.

```
<mx:Repeater dataProvider="{galleryData.lastResult.gallery.images.img}" id="imageRepeater">
```

Figure 9-15. Original dataProvider

To make it work with our videos, change the code to look like Figure 9-16.

```
<mx:Repeater dataProvider="{galleryData.lastResult.gallery.videos.video}" id="imageRepeater">
```

Figure 9-16. Changed dataProvider

You can see that everything stays the same but that instead of images, we put in videos (because that is the way it's named in our XML) and we changed img to video. This tells Flex what kind of file it is.

Altering the file to work with video

For the next section, we can jump back to the Design view so that we can see visually what is happening. The first thing that you will likely notice is that the thumbnail image icon is broken (Figure 9-17).

Figure 9-17. Image component
with broken image icon

The image is broken because we are now trying to bring videos into it instead of images. An Image component does not know how to deal with videos, so we are going to have to replace it with a VideoDisplay component.

8. Delete the existing Image component and replace it with a VideoDisplay component. Scale the VideoDisplay component so that it's 50 by 50 pixels (Figure 9-18).

Figure 9-18. Thumbnails video
in place

9. We need to change many of the same properties settings for this component as we did for the image thumbnails because many of the actions of this video will be the same as those for the image thumbnails. First, set the source of the video to be taken from the repeater (which pulls them from the XML), as shown in Figure 9-19. Also set Auto play to false. This keeps your thumbnail videos from all playing at once and eating up the processor.

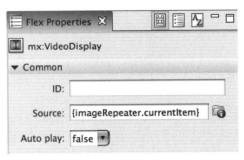

Figure 9-19. VideoDisplay source

10. We can also bring in our rollover effects in the same way as before. In the Category view of the properties for this VideoDisplay component, set the rollOutEffect to {out} and the rollOverEffect to {over}. These are the names of the effects that we created earlier and that were carried over in the MXML file when we copied it (Figure 9-20).

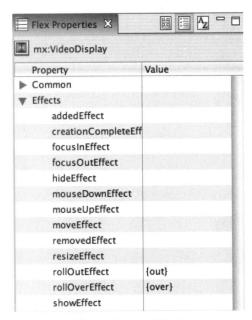

Figure 9-20. Rollover effects on VideoDisplay

11. So far, these are the same changes that we made for the image thumbnails. We'll add the new part, which controls the dragging, to the mouseMove property in the Events section of the Category view (Figure 9-21).

mouseFocusCha|	
mouseMove	**dragIt(event,event.target.getRepeaterItem())**
mouseOut	

Figure 9-21. Adding the dragging function to VideoDisplay

Set this property to dragIt(event, event.target.getRepeaterItem()). We will create this function to manage the drag-and-drop of this video piece.

12. Since we are dealing with videos now, the View Panel Image component must also be changed to a VideoDisplay component. Delete the existing Image component. Put a VideoDisplay component in its place and size it to fill the entire content area of the View Panel (Figure 9-22).

Figure 9-22. Large VideoDisplay

189

13. This component will display our videos when they are dragged onto the View Panel. The only property that we have to assign for this one is the name, so set the ID to myVideo (Figure 9-23).

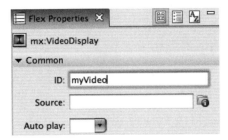

Figure 9-23. Naming the VideoDisplay component

The View Panel will serve as our drop target for our drag-and-drop operation.

14. To make the panel ready to accept the dragged item, we need to set some of its properties. For the View Panel component, set the properties of the dragDrop, dragEnter, and dragExit properties are shown in Figure 9-24. These are functions that we are about to write that control what we want to happen at each of these events.

dragDrop	dragDropHandler(event);
dragEnter	dragEnterHandler(event);
dragExit	dragExitHandler(event);

Figure 9-24. Adding the drag functions

Writing the drag-and-drop functions

To control the drag-and-drop in Flex, we need to create the functions that spell out what we want to do. This is done through ActionScript.

The code is provided as a text file with this chapter's download files, but let's walk through to see how it all works. Jump to the Source view of your project as this is where all ActionScript goes.

ActionScript is generally placed within the <script></script> tags (Figure 9-25).

```
<mx:Script>
        <![CDATA[
            import mx.events.*;

            //import component classes
            import mx.controls.VideoDisplay;
            import mx.containers.Panel;
            //import drag & drop classes
            import mx.events.DragEvent;
            import mx.managers.DragManager;
            import mx.core.*;
```

Figure 9-25. Script tags

The code provided in the text file dragAndDropCode replaces the code that was in these tags previously. This code is generally placed in the MXML file before the MXML tags.

The first piece of code (Figure 9-26) brings in the classes that will be used later.

```
//Handle drag of videos
private function dragIt(event:MouseEvent, value:String):void
{
  // instantiate dragInitiator
  var dragInitiator:VideoDisplay = event.currentTarget as VideoDisplay;

  // instantiate dragSource
  var dragSource:DragSource = new DragSource();
  dragSource.addData(value, 'value');

  // instantiate dragProxy
  var dragProxy:VideoDisplay = new VideoDisplay();
  dragProxy.source = event.currentTarget.source;

  //set size of the thumbnails being dragged
  dragProxy.width = 150 ;
  dragProxy.height = 150 ;

  DragManager.doDrag(dragInitiator, dragSource, event, dragProxy);
}
```

Figure 9-26. Imported classes

Importing just the classes that are needed, as opposed to all possible classes, helps keep the file sizes small. In this case, we are importing the classes used to control the components we use (namely, VideoDisplay and Panel) and the classes that we use to specify what we want our dragging to do.

The next piece of code creates our dragIt function (Figure 9-27). This is the function that we connected to our video thumbnail through its mouseMove property earlier.

```
//Handle drag of videos
private function dragIt(event:MouseEvent, value:String):void
{
  // instantiate dragInitiator
  var dragInitiator:VideoDisplay = event.currentTarget as VideoDisplay;

  // instantiate dragSource
  var dragSource:DragSource = new DragSource();
  dragSource.addData(value, 'value');

  // instantiate dragProxy
  var dragProxy:VideoDisplay = new VideoDisplay();
  dragProxy.source = event.currentTarget.source;

  //set of the thumbanails being dragged
  dragProxy.width = 150 ;
  dragProxy.height = 150 ;

  DragManager.doDrag(dragInitiator, dragSource, event, dragProxy);
}
```

Figure 9-27. Dragging function

This function does a variety of things to control the drag-and-drop of the videos. Let's walk through it piece by piece. The function is called dragIt and is called by the thumbnail videos whenever the user drags a video. The next three pieces of code are all involved in instantiating the objects needed for drag-and-drop. *Instantiate* is a term in object-oriented programming that means to create a specific object that is an instance of a class. So in the first code piece, dragInitiatior, we are creating an instance of the VideoDisplay. We also create a dragSource, which remembers which video is being dragged, and a dragProxy. The dragProxy is the image or video you wish to show as the object is being dragged. You can control the appearance of the dragProxy; in this case, we are setting the size of the video being shown to 150 by 150 pixels, making it larger than the other thumbnails and so bringing attention to it. The DragManager controls what object gets used and when. This function controls what happens to the thumbnails during the dragging. The final piece of the code (Figure 9-28) controls how the drop target responds.

```
//Handle when entering in the drop zone
private function dragEnterHandler(event:DragEvent):void
{
  var dropTarget:Panel=event.currentTarget as Panel;
  if (event.dragSource.hasFormat('value'))
  {
    DragManager.acceptDragDrop(dropTarget);
  }
}

//Handle exiting drop zone
private function dragExitHandler(event:DragEvent):void
{
  var dropTarget:Panel=event.currentTarget as Panel;
}

//Handle dropping target in drop zone
private function dragDropHandler(event:DragEvent):void
{
  var value:String = event.dragSource.dataForFormat('value') as String;

  myVideo.source = value;
  myVideo.play();
}
```

Figure 9-28. Dropping functions

This code consists of three functions, one for each of the possible events when an object is dragged. The first, dragEnterHandler, controls what happens when the thumbnail is dragged onto the drop target (the main video panel). This function checks that the object being dragged is the kind that is expected (in this case, a video). If it is, then it is accepted. Nothing has yet been added for what to do if it is not accepted. The second function, dragExitHandler, controls the events that occur when the thumbnail is dragged back away from the main View Panel. The third controls what happens when the thumbnail is released onto the View Panel. In this case, the appropriate video is placed into the videoDisplay in the View Panel and played. We set these functions to work with the View Panel dragDrop, dragEnter and dragExit properties earlier in step 14. In programming, this is often called *associating* the functions with the properties (Figure 9-29).

dragDrop	dragDropHandler(event);
dragEnter	dragEnterHandler(event);
dragExit	dragExitHandler(event);

Figure 9-29. Dragging functions for thumb VideoDisplay

Figure 9-30 shows the completed project. Make a note of how the video is presented in a different way in each of the stages of the dragging process. In the thumbnails, we show the videos as static; as a video is being dragged, it plays at a larger size than in the thumbnails and is partially transparent; and in the View Panel it plays in the larger size.

Figure 9-30. Final video gallery

Summary

In this chapter you learned two ways of using drag-and-drop in Flex. The first is the simpler method that applies to List components. These allow you to move text across List components simply by enabling them. The second method, referred to as manually adding drag-and-drop, is more involved and ActionScript based. This method provides greater control of the drag-and-drop and allows it to be used on other components.

You also learned how to use videos in place of images in our gallery.

In the next chapter we will look at charting. The built-in charting capabilities of Flex allow complex data visualization and some dramatic effects.

Chapter 10

EXPLORING FLEX CHARTING

What we'll cover in this chapter:

- Building charts
- Animating charts
- Customizing charts

Files used in this chapter:

- FlexCharting-Base.zip
- FlexCharting-Final.zip

You have two options when purchasing Flex Builder: the Standard edition or the Professional edition. The Professional edition contains extra features such as charting and visualization components, the profilers, and the Flex test automation framework. You use the charting tools in Flex Builder to create dynamic and interactive charts from a data set. This chapter explains how to build charts, connect them to data, animate them, and customize them. To follow along, you need to have Flex Builder Professional. You can download a trial of the Professional edition that will allow you to experiment with charting for 30 days.

To see how charting works, let's start with some data. In this case, we will be creating a grade book as it is a data set that is easy to understand. The final product will use a DataGrid to show the raw data and a series of three charts to display the data visually. The final project will look like Figure 10-1.

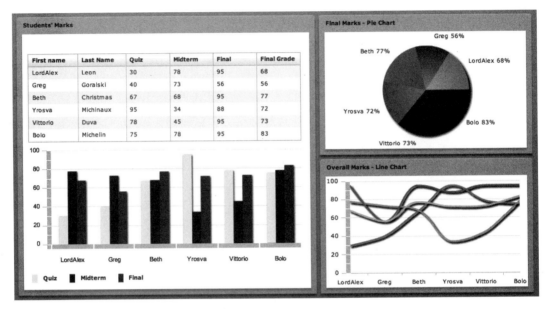

Figure 10-1. Our finished project will look like this.

Importing a project into Flex Builder

So that you can start working with charting right away, in the code download for this book at www.friendsofed.com you'll find a file that holds the basic code and associated files in a prebuilt Flex application called FlexCharting-Base.zip. To start working with the file, import it into Flex Builder.

1. Start by going to this book's page on www.friendsofed.com and downloading the source files for this chapter.

2. Next, in Flex Builder select File ➤ Import ➤ Flex Project (Figure 10-2).

3. In the resulting dialog box, browse to where you saved FlexCharting-Base.zip and select it (Figure 10-3).

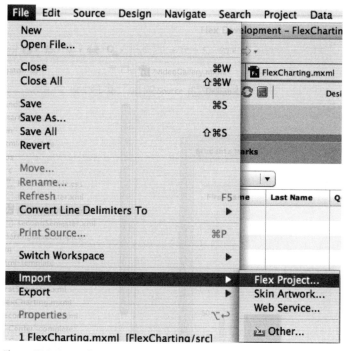

Figure 10-2. Importing our project

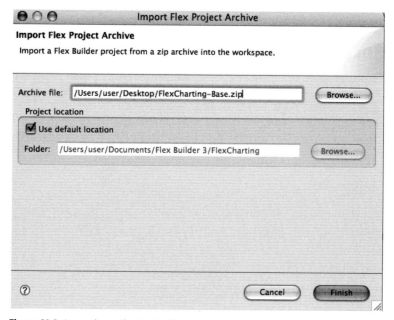

Figure 10-3. Importing a Flex Project from Archive

4. Click Finish to import the project. Flex Builder will then unzip and place all the project files into the default Flex Builder folder. You can follow the same steps to open the completed project FlexCharting-Final.zip to see how it all works when you've finished.

5. Select the MXML file in the Navigator panel to verify that the file has been created (Figure 10-4). Double-click the file to load it.

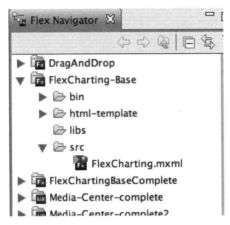

Figure 10-4. Double-click the MXML file.

6. In the Design view, the document will look blank because we haven't added any components. In the Source view, you can see the ActionScript that Flex Builder has created to make this project work. Let's walk through this ActionScript to get a sense of what is happening before we start connecting the charts to the data.

A look at the ActionScript involved

This code (Figure 10-5) uses some of the same techniques that we have used in previous chapters to import XML data. Specifically, it uses the HTTPService to bring in the data and then stores it in the student XMLList. It is the data in student that our DataGrid and Charts components will call. We also have some code that will populate a ComboBox component that will allow us to jump between two different XML files, one called firstSemester.xml and the other called secondSemester.xml (Figure 10-6). Each of the XML files has the names and grades of six students. It is this data that we are charting.

```
<mx:Script>
    <![CDATA[
        // import statements
        import mx.rpc.events.ResultEvent;
        import mx.collections.ArrayCollection;
        import mx.collections.XMLListCollection;
        // this creates an XMLList called 'student' - it will hold the
        // XML data that is brought in from two XML files
        [Bindable]
        private var student:XMLList;
        // the array named 'semester' is used by our ComboBox to select
        // which of the two XML files we want to pull from
        [Bindable]
        private var semester: Array = [ {label:"First Semester",
            data:"firstSemester.xml"}, {label:"Second Semester",
            data:"secondSemester.xml"} ];
        // this function handles data coming from the student XML file
        private function onResult(event:ResultEvent):void
        {
            student = event.result.student;
        }
        // Override the display legend for the PieChart
        // By Overriding the display legend for the PieChart we can
        // better control how the data is presented when the user rolls
        // over a section of the chart.
        private function showStudent(data:Object, field:String,
            index:Number, percentValue:Number):String
        {
            return data.name +" "+data.average + "%";
        }
        // Update data provider for charts
        private function updateData(event:Event):void
        {
            studentData.url = event.target.selectedItem.data;
            studentData.send();
        }
    ]]>
</mx:Script>
```

Figure 10-5. Our ActionScript

```
// The array named 'semester' is used by our ComboBox
// to select which of the two XML files we want to pull data from.

[Bindable]
private var semester: Array = [{label:"First Semester", data:"firstSemester.xml"},
                               {label:"Second Semester", data:"secondSemester.xml"}];
```

Figure 10-6. Variable to be used for our ComboBox

Building the layout

To control the layout, we will be using three panels. The first panel will be largest and will contain the DataGrid and Column Chart. The second and third will contain the Pie Chart and Line Chart.

1. Switch back to the Design view, and drag out three Panel components and arrange them, as shown in Figure 10-7. You do not need to get it exactly the same—a rough estimate is fine.

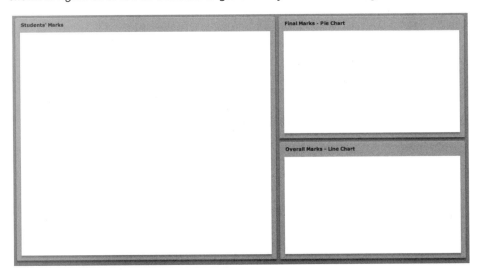

Figure 10-7. Panel layout

For each of the panels, add the appropriate titles in the Title property of the component.

Adding the DataGrid

The DataGrid component is useful for seeing the exact values of a set of data. We'll connect it to our XML files so that we can see the names and marks of all the students. You can find this component in the Controls folder in the Components window.

1. Drag a DataGrid component onto the Students' Marks panel and expand it to fit (Figure 10-8).

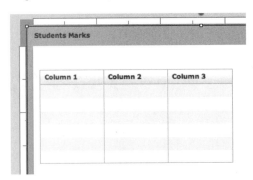

Figure 10-8. Our empty DataGrid

2. Set the ID property of the DataGrid to studentsGrid, so that we can call on it later. In order to place the data from our XML files into this component, set the XMLList that we named {student} as the Data provider (Figure 10-9). Make your DataGrid editable by setting the Editable property to true.

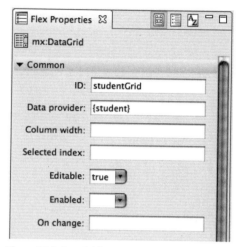

Figure 10-9. DataGrid properties

3. At first the DataGrid comes with generic column names and it does not know which data from the XML file goes where. We need to enter the Source view to change these and guide the data. If you keep the DataGrid component selected when you switch views, the DataGrid code will be automatically highlighted in the Source view (Figure 10-10).

```
<mx:Panel x="10" y="10" width="548" height="492" layout="absolute" title="Students' Marks">
    <mx:DataGrid x="20" y="23" id="studentGrid" dataProvider="{student}">
        <mx:columns>
            <mx:DataGridColumn headerText="Column 1" dataField="col1"/>
            <mx:DataGridColumn headerText="Column 2" dataField="col2"/>
            <mx:DataGridColumn headerText="Column 3" dataField="col3"/>
        </mx:columns>
    </mx:DataGrid>
</mx:Panel>
```

Figure 10-10. DataGrid MXML

4. Each DataGridColumn needs to be changed so that the headerText states what you want each column to be called and that the dataField points to what part of the XML file to put into it. The XML file has the structure shown in Figure 10-11.

```
<students>
    <student>
        <name>LordAlex</name>
        <lastname>Leon</lastname>
        <quiz>70</quiz>
        <midterm>80</midterm>
        <final>90</final>
        <average>96</average>
    </student>
```

Figure 10-11. XML structure

5. Fill in each of the dataField properties to match the tags in the XML file. Change the headerText property to a description of what the column will contain. You can also control the width for each column here so that each column is given enough space by adding a width property to each column. Simply type the property at the end of each line before the closing tag. You will notice that the default DataGrid component only contains three columns, but we need six to contain all of the XML information. To create a new column, copy and paste another three of the DataGrid lines, then fill them in. The final DataGrid MXML should look like Figure 10-12.

```
<mx:Panel x="10" y="10" width="548" height="492" layout="absolute" title="Students' Marks">
    <mx:DataGrid x="20" y="23" id="studentGrid" dataProvider="{student}">
        <mx:columns>
            <mx:DataGridColumn headerText="First name" dataField="name" width="90"/>
            <mx:DataGridColumn headerText="Last Name" dataField="lastname" width="90"/>
            <mx:DataGridColumn headerText="Quiz" dataField="quiz" width="80"/>
            <mx:DataGridColumn headerText="Midterm" dataField="midterm" width="80"/>
            <mx:DataGridColumn headerText="Final" dataField="final" width="80"/>
            <mx:DataGridColumn headerText="Final Grade" dataField="average" width="80"/>
        </mx:columns>
    </mx:DataGrid>
</mx:Panel>
```

Figure 10-12. DataGrid with headerText, dataField, and width properties

6. Switch back to the Design view, and adjust the size of the DataGrid so that it fits well in your panel. We will be adding a ComboBox component above the DataGrid later, so move it down about 30 pixels within the panel.

7. Run the project by clicking the green arrow on the main toolbar. You should see the data from the XML file displayed in the DataGrid (Figure 10-13).

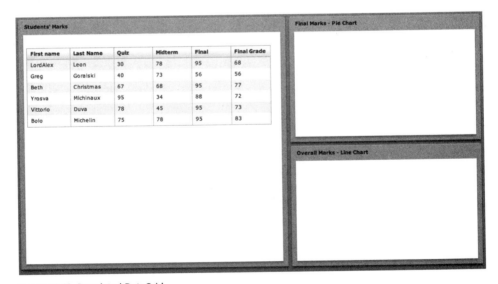

Figure 10-13. Populated DataGrid

Creating a column chart

In your list of possible components, there is a folder called Charts. This folder holds all the different kinds of charts that are available in Flex Builder (Figure 10-14).

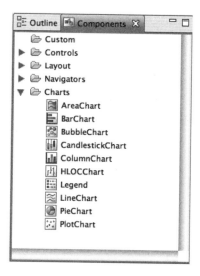

Figure 10-14. Charts in the Components panel

You can see that there is a good variety of charts, and they are all customizable. We will be working with the ColumnChart first.

1. Drag a ColumnChart onto the Students' Marks panel below the DataGrid. As you release the chart, a dialog box will open where you can name the chart and specify the Series elements that it will display. In our case, the elements will be the Quiz, Midterm, and Final marks for our students. Fill in the ID field, and use the Add button to add elements, as shown in Figure 10-15. Also, leave the Include legend check box selected.

Figure 10-15. Create Chart dialog box

2. Once the chart is in position, you can adjust its size. You can also change the size and location of the legend. Depending on the shape of the bounding box around the legend, you can control whether it is to be horizontal or vertical. Figure 10-16 shows our design so far.

Figure 10-16. Chart layout

3. We now need to connect the chart to our data, in the same way we did for the DataGrid. Set the Data provider property for the chart to {student}, set the Type to clustered, and set Show data tips to true (Figure 10-17). Show data tips gives you information about a point in the chart when you roll over it.

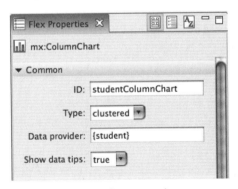

Figure 10-17. ColumnChart properties

4. As we did with the DataGrid, we must tell the chart which data from the XML we want shown where. Switch back to the Source view and set the yField values to the XML fields we want to go in them, as shown in Figure 10-18. The yField values define the height of the columns. So

if the quiz mark for the first student is 60, the value 60 gets sent to the first column of the first student, giving the column a height of 60.

```
<mx:series>
    <mx:ColumnSeries displayName="Quiz" yField="quiz"/>
    <mx:ColumnSeries displayName="Midterm" yField="midterm"/>
    <mx:ColumnSeries displayName="Final" yField="average"/>
</mx:series>
```

Figure 10-18. ColumnChart MXML with yFields

5. To tell the chart what values to place along the x-axis, let's add some new MXML. The MXML showing the horizontal axis categoryField shown in Figure 10-19 adds this to the chart. Copy all three lines of the horizontalAxis tag into your MXML.

```
<mx:ColumnChart x="10" y="176" id="studentColumnChart" height="241" width="503">
    <mx:horizontalAxis>
        <mx:CategoryAxis categoryField="name"/>
    </mx:horizontalAxis>
    <mx:series>
        <mx:ColumnSeries displayName="Quiz" yField="quiz"/>
        <mx:ColumnSeries displayName="Midterm" yField="midterm"/>
        <mx:ColumnSeries displayName="Final" yField="average"/>
    </mx:series>
</mx:ColumnChart>
```

Figure 10-19. ColumnChart MXML with categoryField

6. Run the project to see how the chart looks at this point. You can see in Figure 10-20 that the chart now shows our data clearly.

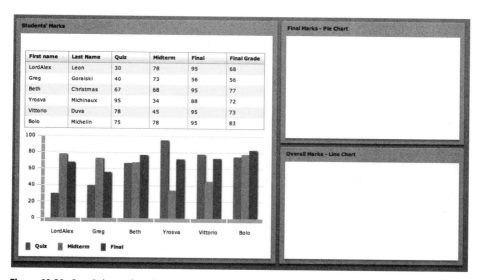

Figure 10-20. Our ColumnChart is now populated.

Controlling the visual appearance of a chart through CSS

The colors and the fonts at this stage are set by Flex Builder. One way to change the appearance of a chart is through CSS. An example CSS file, called BarChartStyle.css, is included within the FlexCharting-Base project that you imported at the beginning of this chapter. If you open the file by double-clicking on it, you can see the form of the CSS for a chart (Figure 10-21).

```
1  /* CSS file */
2  ColumnChart {
3      fontFamily:Arial;
4      fontSize:11;
5      color:#000000;
6      chartSeriesStyles: PCCSeries1, PCCSeries2, PCCSeries3;
7  }
8
9  .PCCSeries1 {
10     fill: #FFFF33;
11 }
12
13 .PCCSeries2 {
14     fill: #0000FF;
15 }
16
17 .PCCSeries3 {
18     fill: #FF0000;
19 }
```

Figure 10-21. ColumnChart CSS

You can see the font is set for the entire chart, and individual colors are set for each series. Notice also that the CSS defines which kind of chart we want to apply this to. To connect this CSS to the chart, add the code in Figure 10-22 to the MXML in the Source view. This is the same technique that we have used in previous examples to connect a CSS file. By convention, this code is placed before the ActionScript in the MXML.

```
<!-- We can customize the charts using css -->
<mx:Style source="BarChartStyle.css"/>
```

Figure 10-22. Adding CSS to our project

Creating a line chart with animation

One of the interesting features about Flex charts is that it is fairly easy to create smooth transitional animations when the data changes. You can have the chart interpolate (gradually move the points on the chart from the current position to the new position), zoom (scale the chart data), and slide (gradually move the points off the chart and then bring them back to the new position).

The easiest of these is the interpolate. To animate a chart, you must first define the animation. This is done in the Source view by creating the tag shown in Figure 10-23. Add this code after the HTTPService and before the panels in the MXML.

```
<mx:SeriesInterpolate id="chartChange" duration="2000"/>
```

Figure 10-23. Interpolate animation

You can see in this tag that it defines the kind of movement (interpolate), gives the animation an ID (chartChange) so that we can call on it, and specifies a duration in milliseconds (in this case 2000, or 2 seconds). Add this tag to your MXML—we will be coming back to call on it once we create our line chart.

1. First we need to create the line chart. In the Design view, drag a LineChart component onto the panel named Overall Marks – Line Chart. We will be going through much the same process to create this one as we did with the column chart.

2. When you release your chart, you will see the Create Chart dialog box. Add the elements shown in Figure 10-24. We will not need the legend for this chart, so deselect the Include legend check box.

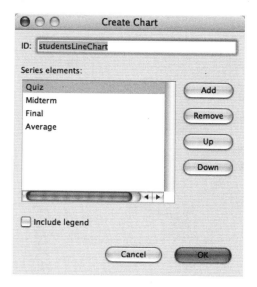

Figure 10-24. Use these settings in the Create Chart dialog box.

3. Adjust the size of the chart so that it fits in your panel and enter {student} for the Data provider property (Figure 10-25). Set the Show data tips attribute to true.

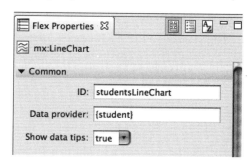

Figure 10-25. Line chart properties

4. As we did for the column chart, switch to the Source view and add the yField and horizontalAxis information, as shown in Figure 10-26.

```
<mx:LineChart x="0" y="0" id="studentsLineChart" width="368" height="197" dataProvider="{student}"
    showDataTips="true">
    <mx:horizontalAxis>
        <mx:CategoryAxis categoryField="name"/>
    </mx:horizontalAxis>
    <mx:series>
        <mx:LineSeries displayName="Quiz" yField="quiz"/>
        <mx:LineSeries displayName="Midterm" yField="midterm"/>
        <mx:LineSeries displayName="Final" yField="final"/>
        <mx:LineSeries displayName="Average" yField="average"/>
    </mx:series>

</mx:LineChart>
```

Figure 10-26. Line chart MXML

If we have a look at our project so far, we can see how each line represents an assignment. Run the project by clicking the green arrow in the main toolbar. Rolling over a point in the chart will tell you the exact mark and who received it (Figure 10-27).

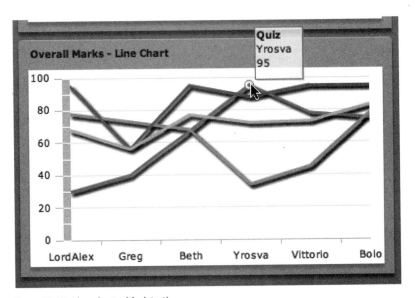

Figure 10-27. Line chart with data tips

If the data were to change right now, the change would happen without a transition. You can try this by changing one of the grades in the DataGrid (this is why we made it editable). Just click on a grade and enter a new value. To make the transition smooth, let's connect this chart to the interpolate animation we created earlier.

5. Return to the Source view for this chart and modify the line series, as shown in Figure 10-28.

```
<mx:LineChart x="0" y="0" id="studentsLineChart" width="368" height="197" dataProvider="{student}"
    showDataTips="true">
    <mx:horizontalAxis>
            <mx:CategoryAxis categoryField="name"/>
        </mx:horizontalAxis>
    <mx:series>
        <mx:LineSeries displayName="Quiz" yField="quiz" showDataEffect="{chartChange}"/>
        <mx:LineSeries displayName="Midterm" yField="midterm" showDataEffect="{chartChange}"/>
        <mx:LineSeries displayName="Final" yField="final" showDataEffect="{chartChange}"/>
        <mx:LineSeries displayName="Average" yField="average" showDataEffect="{chartChange}"/>
    </mx:series>

</mx:LineChart>
```

Figure 10-28. Line chart MXML with animation

6. The addition of showDataEffect = "{chartChange}" tells the chart to use the animation that we previously defined as chartChange when data is changed. While we are here, we can modify the kind of line that gets used. Let's make the line curve (as opposed to being straight) by adding form="curve" for each series, as shown in Figure 10-29.

```
<mx:LineChart x="0" y="0" id="studentsLineChart" width="368" height="197" dataProvider="{student}"
    showDataTips="true">
    <mx:horizontalAxis>
            <mx:CategoryAxis categoryField="name"/>
        </mx:horizontalAxis>
    <mx:series>
        <mx:LineSeries displayName="Quiz" yField="quiz" form="curve" showDataEffect="{chartChange}"/>
        <mx:LineSeries displayName="Midterm" yField="midterm" form="curve" showDataEffect="{chartChange}"/>
        <mx:LineSeries displayName="Final" yField="final" form="curve" showDataEffect="{chartChange}"/>
        <mx:LineSeries displayName="Average" yField="average" form="curve" showDataEffect="{chartChange}"/>
    </mx:series>

</mx:LineChart>
```

Figure 10-29. Line chart MXML with form curve

Looking at our project now, we can see that the lines are curved and changing the data in the DataGrid causes a smooth two-second change in the position of the point. As an added bonus, when the page loads our chart grows from the base.

7. Now that we have created the transition, we can use the same transition on any of our other charts by adding the same code to the series. Figure 10-30 shows how this would look for the column chart.

```
<mx:ColumnChart x="10" y="197" id="studentColumnChart" dataProvider="{student}" width="502" height=
    <mx:horizontalAxis>
        <mx:CategoryAxis categoryField="name"/>
    </mx:horizontalAxis>
    <mx:series>
        <mx:ColumnSeries displayName="Quiz" yField="quiz" showDataEffect="{chartChange}"/>
        <mx:ColumnSeries displayName="Midterm" yField="midterm" showDataEffect="{chartChange}"/>
        <mx:ColumnSeries displayName="Final" yField="average" showDataEffect="{chartChange}"/>
    </mx:series>
</mx:ColumnChart>
```

Figure 10-30. Column chart MXML with animation

Creating a pie chart

The last kind of chart we will be creating is the pie chart.

1. Drag a PieChart component onto the Final Marks – Pie Chart panel. Again, the Create Chart dialog box opens. For the PieChart component, we will only be looking at the final average of each student, so complete the dialog box as shown in Figure 10-31. Be sure to deselect the Include legend check box. We won't need a legend on this chart as it will be clear when the user rolls over the individual pies.

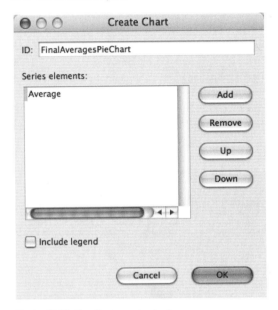

Figure 10-31. Creating our pie chart

2. Adjust the size of your component and set the Data provider **property to** {student} **and the** Show data tips **attribute to** true (Figure 10-32).

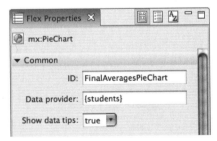

Figure 10-32. Our pie chart's properties

3. We need to tell the chart which piece of information we want displayed in this chart, as we have done before, in the source MXML, as shown in Figure 10-33.

```
<mx:PieChart x="0" y="0" id="FinalAveragesPieChart" width="368" height="207" dataProvider="{student}"
    showDataTips="true">
    <mx:series>
        <mx:PieSeries displayName="Average" field="average" labelPosition="outside"/>
    </mx:series>
```

Figure 10-33. Pie chart MXML specifying the label position

Since a pie chart does not have x or y coordinates, the property is called `field`, as opposed to `yField` for the other charts. We have also added a `labelPosition` property here that will tell us what the data is along the outside of the pie chart.

Running our project shows us what our pie chart will look like (Figure 10-34).

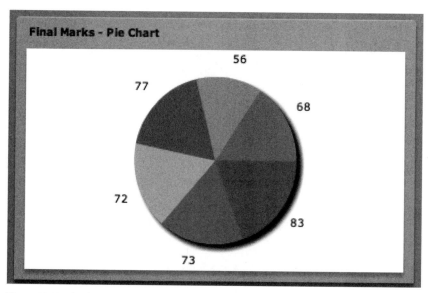

Figure 10-34. Pie chart with labels

Unfortunately, our labels don't tell us enough information for this chart to be effective. We need to put more than one of the values from our DataGrid into each label, specifically the students' names and their averages (right now it is just the averages). We do this by creating a function that controls what is seen in the label. Figure 10-35 shows the ActionScript label function showStudent, which overrides the existing label and gives it the name of the student, a space, the average, and the percent symbol.

```
//Override the display legend for the PieChart
private function showStudent(data:Object, field:String, index:Number, percentValue:Number):String
{
    return data.name +" "+data.average + "%";
}
```

Figure 10-35. ShowStudent label function

4. To add this function to the pie chart, add labelFunction="showStudent" to the PieSeries MXML (Figure 10-36).

```
<mx:PieChart x="0" y="0" id="FinalAveragesPieChart" width="368" height="207" dataProvider="{student}"
    showDataTips="true">
    <mx:series>
        <mx:PieSeries displayName="Average" field="average" labelPosition="outside" labelFunction="showStudent" />
    </mx:series>
```

Figure 10-36. Pie chart MXML with the ShowStudent label function

Looking at our pie chart now, you can see that it is a good deal clearer (Figure 10-37).

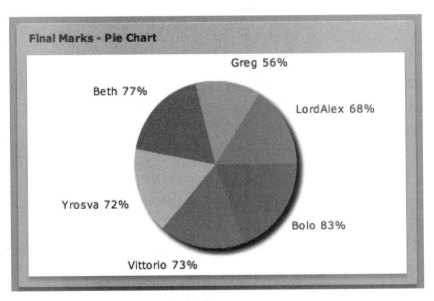

Figure 10-37. Pie chart with informative labels

5. The pie chart gives us an opportunity to try another form of chart customization. We can modify the colors, and what's more we can make them gradients, in the MXML. We'll add a series of gradients inside a fill tag, as shown in Figure 10-38. Add this code after the `<mx:PieSeries>` tag.

```
<!-- We can add colors and gradients by means of mxml tags -->
<mx:fills>
<mx:RadialGradient>
    <mx:entries>
        <mx:GradientEntry color="#E9C836"/>
        <mx:GradientEntry color="#AA9127"/>
    </mx:entries>
</mx:RadialGradient>
<mx:RadialGradient>
    <mx:entries>
        <mx:GradientEntry color="#A1AECF"/>
        <mx:GradientEntry color="#47447A"/>
    </mx:entries>
</mx:RadialGradient>
<mx:RadialGradient>
    <mx:entries>
        <mx:GradientEntry color="#339933"/>
        <mx:GradientEntry color="#339998"/>
    </mx:entries>
</mx:RadialGradient>
<mx:RadialGradient>
    <mx:entries>
        <mx:GradientEntry color="#6FB35F"/>
        <mx:GradientEntry color="#497B54"/>
    </mx:entries>
</mx:RadialGradient>
<mx:RadialGradient>
    <mx:entries>
        <mx:GradientEntry color="#FF0000"/>
        <mx:GradientEntry color="#500000"/>
    </mx:entries>
</mx:RadialGradient>
<mx:RadialGradient>
    <mx:entries>
        <mx:GradientEntry color="#0033FF"/>
        <mx:GradientEntry color="#000066"/>
    </mx:entries>
</mx:RadialGradient>
</mx:fills>
```

Figure 10-38. Pie chart MXML with gradients

This is a very code-centric way of designing, but it does give a good effect (Figure 10-39). In this example, the first gradient entry defines the inner color and the second defines the outside color.

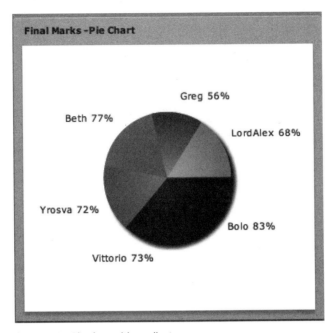

Figure 10-39. Pie chart with gradients

Adding a second set of data

To see the transitional effects more dramatically, we have added a second XML file with more data. This one holds the grades for the second semester. To switch from one semester to another, we will be using a ComboBox.

1. Place a ComboBox above the DataGrid. Set the Data provider for the ComboBox to {semester} (Figure 10-40). This is a variable that we created in the ActionScript that holds the names of the two XML files. Set Selected index to 0; this makes the ComboBox start with the first option selected. Set Enabled to true.

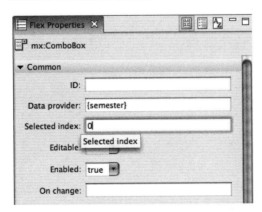

Figure 10-40. ComboBox properties

2. To make it respond, enter updateData(event) for the close event (Figure 10-41). You can find the updateData event in the Category view of the Flex properties for the ComboBox in the Events folder.

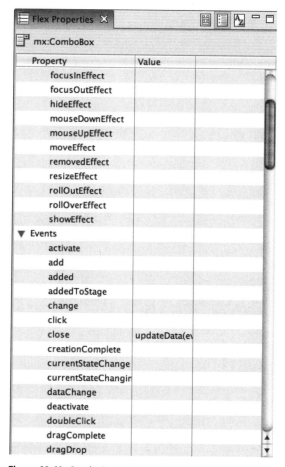

Figure 10-41. ComboBox event properties

Summary

The charts in Flex are a powerful tool that you can use to present data in a dynamic and compelling way. We looked at two major ways of modifying the look of the charts: using CSS and adding fills directly to the MXML.

The charts can be animated through interpolate, zoom, or slide, and labels can be modified to better represent a chart. In the next chapter, we'll look at forms, data validation, and the Accordion component.

Chapter 11

CREATING FORMS: THE "WILL FLEX FOR FOOD" REGISTRATION PAGE

What we'll cover in this chapter:

- Accordion component
- Data validation

Files used in this chapter:

- CH11-WillFlexForFood.zip

One of the real strengths of Flex is the ease of form creation. Forms are a common technique in web design when you want to get a lot of information from the user. They come up whenever you register for a site, send feedback, or buy something online. Often more complicated forms come in multiple screens. If you are getting set up for a social networking site, for example, you often go through a profile information form, followed by an interests form, followed by a contact information form. One of the frustrating things with traditional HTML-based forms is that, since they are contained in distinct HTML pages that are loaded individually, it is difficult to go back and change information without losing what you have already written. Flex makes it easy to get a form with multiple stages created in such a way that the user can flip back to change any previous information. Flex can also do some really useful things with the information, such as validating that it is correct.

Flex does this through the use of some fairly complicated components, such as the Accordion component and the tabNavigator component. For our exercise, we will use the Accordion component to create a three-step registration form—the form a user would use to join the fictional "Will Flex for Food" freelance designer network.

You can see the final example in Figure 11-1.

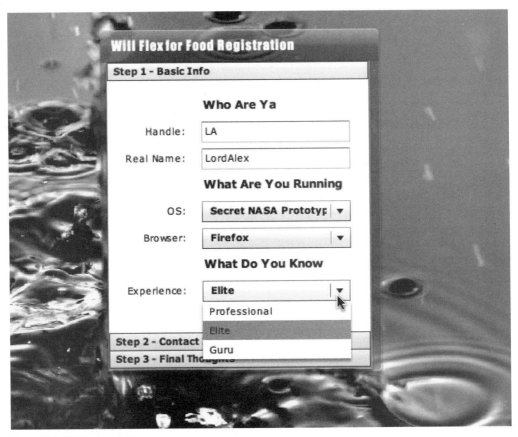

Figure 11-1. Finished project

Getting started

In this chapter we will create a form from scratch in three steps. We will be looking at the layout and validation of information in the form, but we won't connect the project to a database.

1. Start with a new Flex project (Figure 11-2).

Figure 11-2. Creating a new Flex application

2. Name the project CH11-FlexForms and click Finish (Figure 11-3). Flex creates a default MXML file called main.mxml.

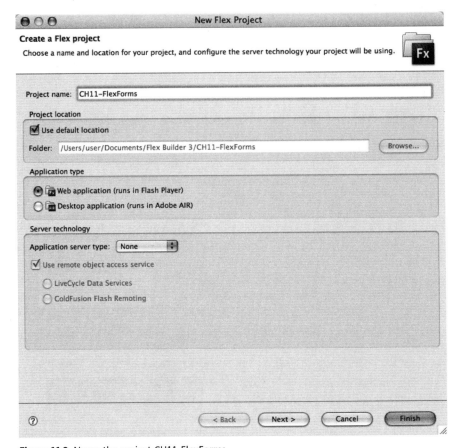

Figure 11-3. Name the project CH11-FlexForms.

3. Select the Design view in the MXML editor.

4. Start by placing a Panel component in the middle of our MXML editor. This Panel will serve to frame our form and help us control the layout (Figure 11-4).

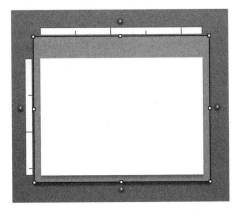

Figure 11-4. Panel component

5. Type mainPanel for the ID and for the Title type Will Flex for Food Registration, as shown in Figure 11-5.

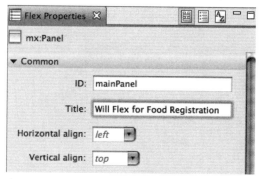

Figure 11-5. Give the panel an ID and title.

6. We want the form to stay centered in the browser window regardless of size and we want the Panel to be large enough to hold our information. In this case, 400 by 400 is a good size. To keep the form centered, set the layout handles to Center (Figure 11-6).

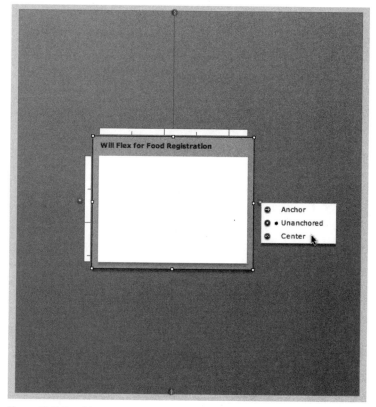

Figure 11-6. Panel layout

Adding the Accordion component

You'll find the Accordion component in the Navigators folder of the Components panel (Figure 11-7). This set of components is useful for moving through larger amounts of data where space is limited.

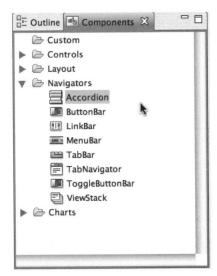

Figure 11-7. Navigators folder in Components panel

7. Drag an Accordion component onto the panel we have just created (Figure 11-8).

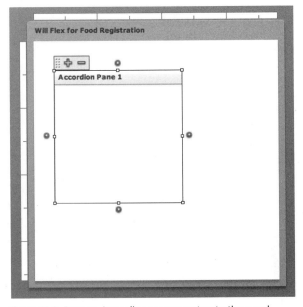

Figure 11-8. Drag an Accordion component onto the panel.

8. Keep a close eye on the Properties panel when working with accordions as you will have two sets of properties depending on what is selected. If the entire Accordion is selected, as shown in Figure 11-8, then the properties that are presented are for the Accordion as a whole. These properties include the ID and the layout of the component along with some styling (Figure 11-9). If just the display area of the Accordion is selected, then the properties of the component in the display area (a canvas by default) are shown.

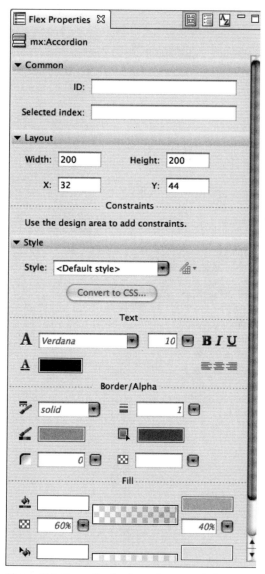

Figure 11-9. Properties for Accordion as a whole

9. Add an ID of MyAccordion so that our Accordion is identified. We won't be using this, but it is good practice to add an ID to all components so that they can be modified by code at a later time.

223

10. Drag the edges of the Accordion so that it takes up the entire display area of the panel. You can also set the height and width to 100% to make the Accordion take up the entire display area of the panel (Figure 11-10).

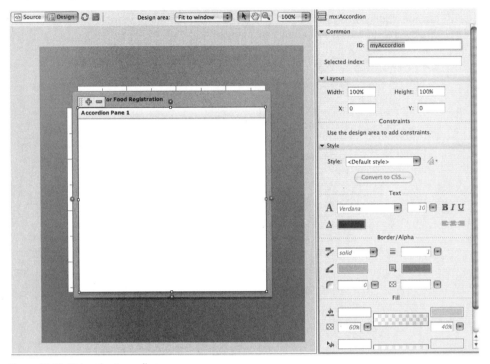

Figure 11-10. Sizing the Accordion

If you accidentally select just the white display area of the Accordion (which selects just an individual pane), click to the left of the plus sign to select the entire Accordion again. This is where the cursor is in Figure 11-11.

Figure 11-11. Selecting the entire Accordion

Adding panes to the Accordion

To increase the number of panes in the Accordion, click the plus sign in the top-left corner. This brings up the Insert Pane dialog box, which allows you to create a label for the Accordion and to set the container type (Figure 11-12). The container for an Accordion pane is the layout component that is held in the pane to organize the layout of the content that you place into it. The pane that is created automatically when you create the Accordion is labeled Accordion Pane 1 and has a canvas component as the container.

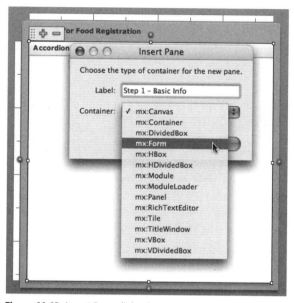

Figure 11-12. Insert Pane dialog box

11. Create three new panes by clicking the plus sign in the top-left corner of the Accordion component. Name the panes Step 1 – Basic Info, Step 2 – Contact Info, and Step 3 – Final Thoughts. Set Form as the container for each pane.

12. As best practice, create an ID for each pane, Step1, Step2, and Step3.

13. Remove the pane that was created automatically with the Accordion (labeled Accordion Pane 1) by selecting this pane and clicking the minus sign in the top-left corner of the Accordion component. Your resulting Accordion will look like Figure 11-13.

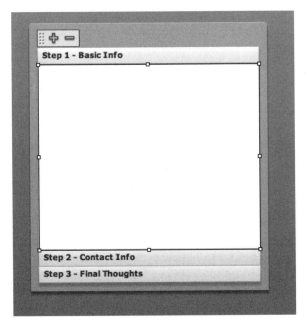

Figure 11-13. Accordion with all panes

We have now created three distinct steps in the Accordion. The white area below each step name is the content area for each pane. Running the project at this point will give you a sense of how the Accordion works. When you click the title area of each pane, it shows the content area associated with it, while keeping the order of the panes consistent. A transition is added to the Accordion by default to give a better effect.

Adding content

You can drop components directly onto the content area of each pane. Using the Form component as the container in each pane helps us quickly create the layout for this example.

14. Select Step 1 – Basic Info to show the content area for the first pane.

15. Drag a FormHeading component onto this area. Notice that regardless of where in the area you place it, the component moves to the top left. This is an example of the layout help that a Form component gives us.

16. For the Label of this FormHeading, type Who are ya. For best practice, for the ID, type WhoAreYa (Figure 11-14).

17. Drag a TextInput component below the FormHeading. Notice that, because we are laying this content onto a Form component, the TextInput is automatically placed inside a FormItem. This gives our TextInput a label along the left and helps with layout. For the Label of the FormItem, enter Handle: and for the ID, type Handle (Figure 11-15).

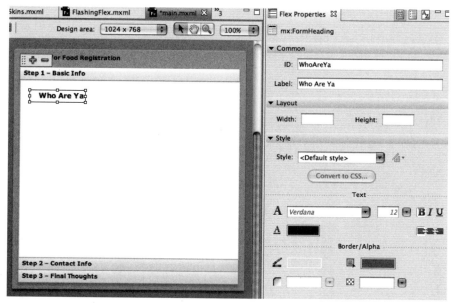

Figure 11-14. Pane with Form heading

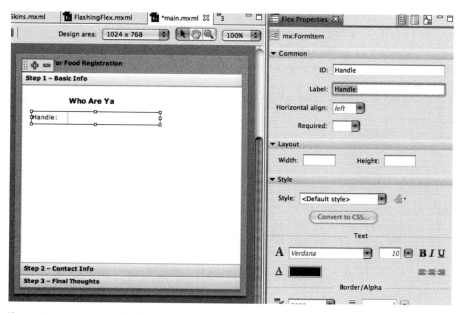

Figure 11-15. FormItem with TextInput added

18. Repeat step 17 to create a FormItem and TextInput for the user's Real Name.

Adding combo boxes

In the same way that it worked with the TextInput component, adding a ComboBox to the form creates a label next to it. This is because the ComboBox gets placed into a FormItem.

19. Repeat steps 15, 16, and 17 with the FormHeadings and ComboBoxes to create the layout shown in Figure 11-16.

Figure 11-16. Labels and TextInput added

20. Give the ComboBox components the IDs osCombo, browserCombo, and experienceCombo.

We will be using ActionScript to create the options in each of the ComboBoxes. We'll do this by creating an array that holds the label for each of the options; see Figure 11-17 for the code.

```
<mx:Script>
    <![CDATA[
        //set dataProviders for the OS, browser and experience comboBoxes
        [Bindable]
        public var os: Array = [   {label:"Windows", data:1},
                                   {label:"Mac OS X", data:2},
                                   {label:"Linux", data:3},
                                   {label:"Secret NASA Prototype", data:4}
                               ];
        [Bindable]
        public var browser: Array = [   {label:"Explorer", data:1},
                                        {label:"Firefox", data:2},
                                        {label:"Safari", data:3}
                                    ];
        [Bindable]
        public var experience: Array = [ {label:"Professional", data:1},
                                         {label:"Elite", data:2},
                                         {label:"Guru", data:3}
                                       ];
    ]]>
</mx:Script>
```

Figure 11-17. ActionScript for populating ComboBoxes

As you can see in Figure 11-17, we are creating three variables: os, browser, and experience. Each of these variables is an array. As we discussed in Chapter 7, an array is a kind of variable that can hold multiple pieces of information. In each array, we create a set of data by placing the label and the data that is associated with it in curly brackets. The entire data set for the array is surrounded by square brackets. We place all of the code in a Script tag to separate it from the MXML.

21. Add this script to your MXML in the Source view above the Panel now.

22. Jumping back to the Design view, connect these arrays to the ComboBoxes by placing the name of the array, surrounded by curly brackets, into the Data provider property of the ComboBoxes (Figure 11-18). Each of the ComboBoxes has its own array, with the array os populating the osCombo, the browser array populating the browserCombo, and the experience array populating the experienceCombo.

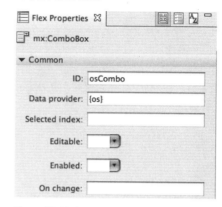

As you connect the arrays, the width of the ComboBox will adjust automatically and will need to be reset.

23. Run the application to see how the ComboBoxes are populated.

Figure 11-18. Data provider for ComboBox set

Working with validation

Now that the first step of our form is complete, we can go on to Step 2 – Contact Info. To start placing the content for the second step, click on the Step 2 – Contact Info label on the Accordion. This will hide the content area of the first step and open the content area of the second step (Figure 11-19).

Figure 11-19. Pane 2 selected

Here we will again be placing TextInput components, which automatically get placed into a FormItem component, but this time we will be taking the extra step of making sure that the text the user enters looks correct. The Form component was added into the content area of the Accordion when the Accordion panel was created. Form should have been the setting at that point.

24. Add a TextInput component. Type a FormItem label as well as a label for users to enter their e-mail address. Make sure that you give the TextInput an ID of email (Figure 11-20).

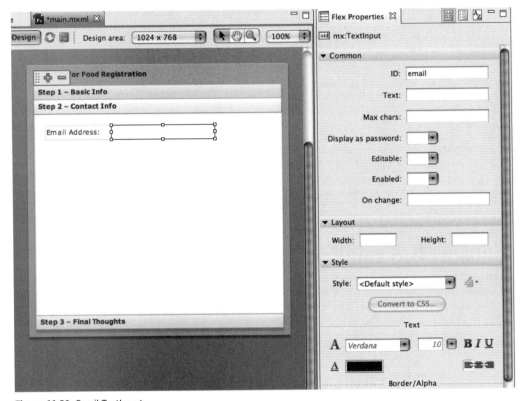

Figure 11-20. Email TextInput

Although we do not know what e-mail address is going to be placed into this field, we do know that there are certain rules about the format of an e-mail address. Flex makes it fairly easy to check that the format is correct and let users know if they've made an error. This is done through a validator, in this case an e-mail validator.

A validator is an MXML tag that checks the format of a certain piece of information. For this example, it looks like Figure 11-21.

```
<mx:EmailValidator id="emailVal" source="{email}" property="text"/>
```

Figure 11-21. E-mail validator

Place this tag in the Source view of your MXML editor before the mx:Panel tag. It consists of an id (so that we can call on it later), a source (the component you want to check), and a property (the property of the component you want to check).

25. Add this MXML tag now and run the application.

In this example, if you enter some text that is not in the format of an e-mail address into this field, it will be highlighted in red (Figure 11-22).

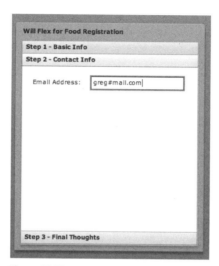

Figure 11-22. An error in e-mail formatting will be highlighted.

Hover your cursor over the component to see a suggested fix for the error (Figure 11-23).

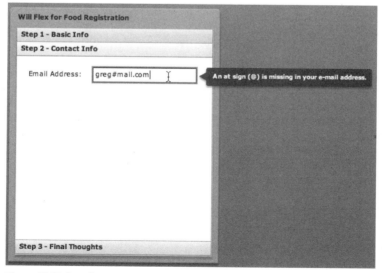

Figure 11-23. E-mail error explained

231

26. Add two more similar labels and TextInput components for the address and postal code (Figure 11-24).

27. The postal code is another example of a field that must be validated. Give this TextInput an ID of zipAndPostalCode. The validation tag for the postal code is similar to the one created for the e-mail, but with a bit extra (Figure 11-25).

```
<mx:ZipCodeValidator
    source="{zipAndPostalCode}"
    property="text"
    domain="US or Canada"
    wrongCAFormatError="The Canadian Postal Code must be formatted A1B 2C3"
    />
```

Figure 11-24. Adding the address and postal code

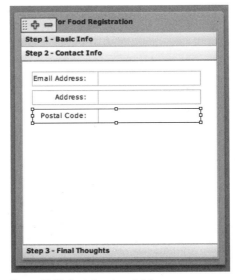

Figure 11-25. Postal code validator

You can see in Figure 11-25 that the source is set to be the id of the TextInput component, and the property is set to the text property of that component. This is the same overall structure we used for the e-mail. But since there are different kinds of postal code formats depending on the country, we added the domain field to include the ones that we want to work with. The wrongCAFormatError property allows you to set your own custom error message. In this case, we have typed The Canadian Postal Code must be formatted 'A1B 2C3'.

Passwords

We treat passwords slightly differently from other contact info, as they should not display the letters that are being typed in.

28. Create a fourth TextInput and Label set below the postal code in the Design view for the password. For this TextInput, for the ID, type password, and set the Display as password property to true (Figure 11-26).

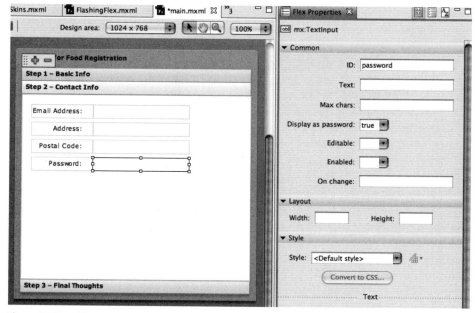

Figure 11-26. Adding the password

This will now hide the password as the user types it in (Figure 11-27), replacing each character with an asterisk.

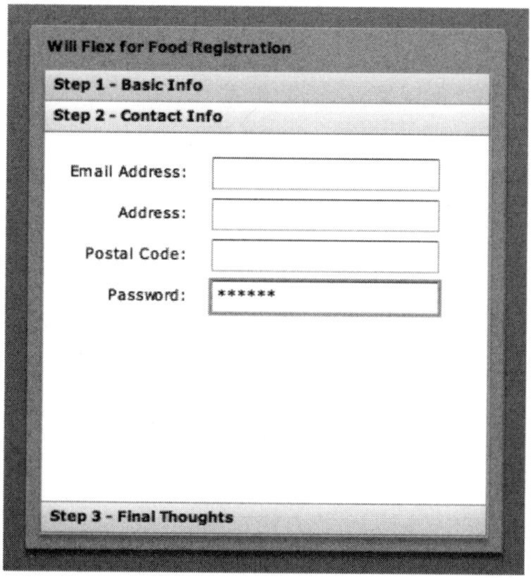

Figure 11-27. Asterisks will replace the password the user types in.

Filling the Final Thoughts pane

The third step of our Accordion will give the user a chance to add longer comments.

29. For the third pane of this example, Step 3 – Final Thoughts, we will be providing the user with some space to leave final comments. Begin by selecting the content area of the third pane (Figure 11-28).

Figure 11-28. Select the third pane.

30. On this pane, place a TextArea for comments, so that users can tell us how intuitive they found our form, and a Submit button. If this application were connected to a database, the Submit button would send the information that was provided to the server. Placing the Submit button on the form will give it a label. We can set this label to be blank (Figure 11-29).

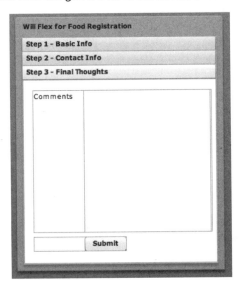

Figure 11-29. Third pane content

Styling your Accordion

You can add CSS to an Accordion in the same way we did in Chapter 2. This is a very efficient way to change the appearance of the component. The Accordion has similar properties to the other components we have looked at previously. It also has one unique property: Open Duration. Open Duration allows you to define how long the transition between the panes takes (Figure 11-30).

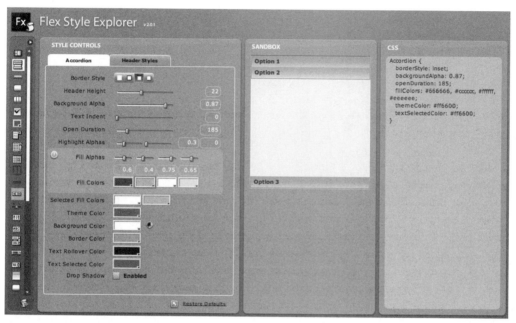

Figure 11-30. Style Explorer for Accordion

Summary

In this chapter you learned how to use Flex to create intuitive, compact forms to obtain information from users. The advantage of using the Accordion component in Flex to create forms is that it can present multiple steps of a registration without separate distinct pages. This makes it easy for a user to move back and forth through the pages.

A second key advantage to creating forms in Flex is the data validation. Validation enables us to check the formatting of the information that the user provides. Using validation gives an immediate response to the user and catches errors quickly.

In the next chapter, we will begin working with Adobe Integrated Runtime (AIR) to create desktop applications that can access the Internet.

Chapter 12

FLEX AND AIR

What we'll cover in this chapter:

- Creating AIR applications
- Accessing files on the desktop
- Creating a custom application shape

Files used in this chapter:

- MediaCenter-start.zip
- MediaCenter-stage1Compete.zip
- MediaCenter-stage2Compete.zip

With the development of Adobe Integrated Runtime (AIR), the possibilities for what you can create with Flex open wider than ever before. In a nutshell, AIR allows you to create your applications in such a way that they live on the user's computer, like Apple Mail or Microsoft Word, as opposed to residing on a web server. That way, the application has the ability to keep working when the user's computer is not connected to the network, a greater ability to remember settings, and easier access to the user's local files (users can even drag a file from their desktop directly into the application). When Internet access is available, the application can pull information in the background and store it for later. These are hybrid applications, mixing the idea of a desktop application with a web application, and they allow you to build using the same tools that you are used to, such as Flash, Ajax, Flex, HTML, or PDFs, and then deploy cross-platform. You do not have to worry about what kind of computer your application will be installed on—AIR works on both PCs and Macs, and a version is planned for Linux. You can build applications much faster than you could using traditional desktop applications while maintaining a small application footprint. The possibilities are very exciting.

To explore how AIR applications work, we will create a media center that will play a variety of media (images, sound, and video) directly from your desktop (Figure 12-1).

Figure 12-1. Completed AIR project

Creating a new AIR application

AIR comes as a part of Flex Builder 3. This includes the Software Developer Kit (SDK) and the actual AIR runtime. The runtime is the framework that allows you to run AIR applications. This needs to be installed only once onto any computer that will be running AIR applications. Therefore, the footprint for the applications themselves is kept small. If you need the AIR SDK or the AIR runtime, you can find them on the main AIR page at http://www.adobe.com/go/air.

1. Create a new Flex project (Figure 12-2) and set the application type to Desktop Application (runs in Adobe AIR). Name the project Media-Center and click Finish.

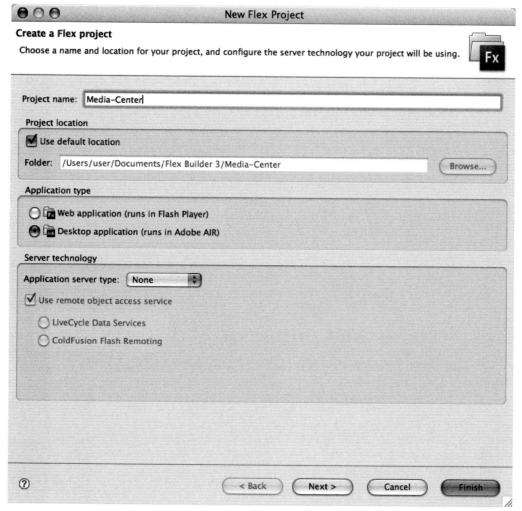

Figure 12-2. Creating a new AIR project

Notice that an extra file is automatically created. We have the MXML file named main.mxml, but we also have main-app.xml. This is the application descriptor file, and it controls how the project is presented. The application descriptor file deals with the default parameters for the AIR application, such as its name, initial color, and shortcut icon. We will be looking closely at this file in the second part of this chapter. For now, it is important to notice this file and not to change its name.

The MXML file is called main.mxml because there is a hyphen in our project name. If there are no hyphens or spaces in a project name, the MXML and the application's descriptor file are assigned the same name as the application. In the case of the application's descriptor file, it is the project name followed by -app.xml (see Figure 12-3).

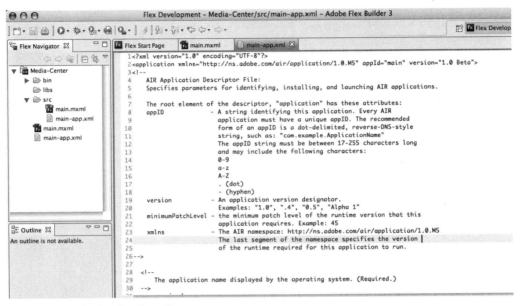

Figure 12-3. Application descriptor file

Since this exercise uses a good deal of ActionScript to create its functionality, you can either open the file MediaCenter-start.zip from the code download for this book at www.friendsofed.com, or you can add the code manually as we go along. MediaCenter-start.zip contains the ActionScript but none of the MXML. We will be looking at all of the ActionScript as we move through the exercise.

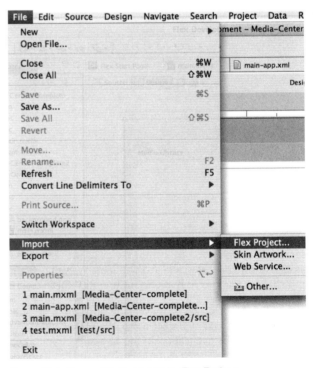

2. Import MediaCenter-start.zip. Copy the file from the website to your desktop. You import an archived project by selecting File ➤ Import ➤ Flex Project (Figure 12-4). At this point, click Browse to find the archived file and then click Finish.

Figure 12-4. Choose File ➤ Import ➤ Flex Project.

Building the Media Center layout

The Media Center layout consists of an Image component, a Video Display component, and a FileSystemTree component. The FileSystemTree component is specifically built for use with AIR. It allows you to access the files on your computer using the same intuitive technique that most file browsers do. We will place the FileSystemTree component on a Panel component to make its layout easier. We will also add a Text component to tell us what kind of file is being shown and to let us know when a file is not recognized. The application's size is the default 800 pixels by 600 pixels.

Figure 12-5 shows the Media Center before styling.

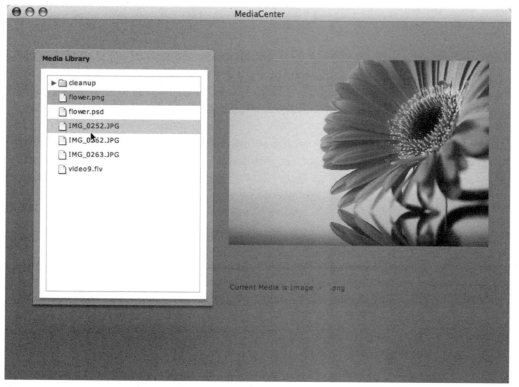

Figure 12-5. Media Center before styling

   3. In the Design view of Flex Builder, drag out a Panel component.

This panel will hold the FileSystemTree so it needs to be large enough to show the files on your desktop.

   4. For the panel specify Width as 310 and Height as 450. Setting the layout constraints along the middle (as shown in Figure 12-6) keeps the panel stationary relative to the center when the size of the window is adjusted.

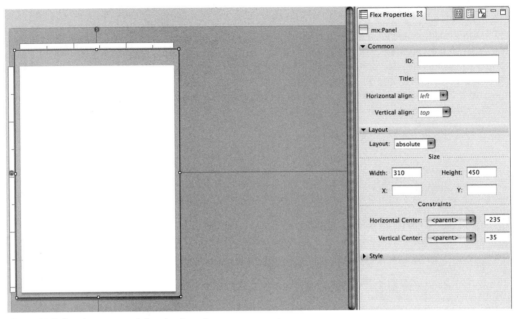

Figure 12-6. Panel component showing layout

5. Set the ID of this panel to `mediaPanel` and the Label to `Media Library`.

6. Drag a FileSystemTree component onto the Panel.

The FileSystemTree component can be found in a folder in the Components navigator that was added when you installed the AIR SDK (Figure 12-7). This folder holds the components that are specific to AIR applications.

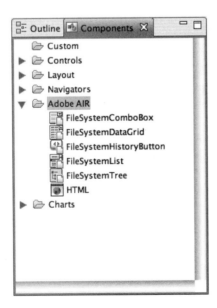

Figure 12-7. FileSystemTree in Components list

7. Set the layout constraints for the FileSystemTree as shown in Figure 12-8. This will allow the FileSystemTree to stay consistent with the Panel component, with a 10-pixel border. For the ID, type tree.

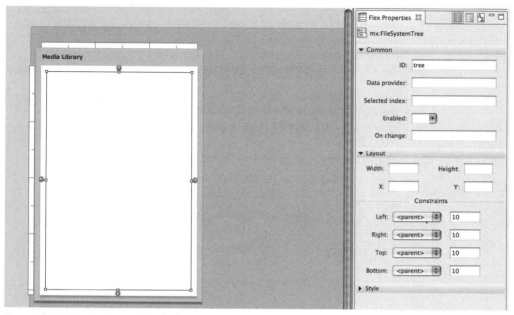

Figure 12-8. FileSystemTree within the Panel component

Much of our interaction within this Media Center is focused on the FileSystemTree component, so it is no surprise that much of the ActionScript is based on this component. Now is a good time for you to enter the ActionScript if you are working from a new document or to examine the ActionScript if you are working from the provided MediaCenter-Start.zip file.

8. Switch over to the Source view in the MXML Editor.

The ActionScript

As with all Flex Builder applications, we begin by creating the Script tags, below the application tags, before the components tags. Below this we list the ActionScript libraries we want to import (Figure 12-9).

```
3  <mx:Script>
4      <![CDATA[
5          //import the File library which we need to navigate directories
6          import flash.filesystem.File;
7          import flash.media.Sound;
8          import flash.media.SoundChannel;
9          import mx.controls.videoClasses.VideoPlayer
10
```

Figure 12-9. Imported file libraries

243

The first of these, flash.filesystem.file, allows us to navigate through the directories on our computer. The following three give us control over our video and sound files.

The function initTree, shown in Figure 12-10, sets our FileSystemTree component to point to the desktop of the user. This function works for both Mac and PC.

```
//Initialize the tree and open the myMedia directory
public function initTree( ):void
{
//Point to user desktop
  tree.directory = File.desktopDirectory;
  }
//
```

Figure 12-10. The initTree function

We will be setting up the function getDetails (see Figure 12-11) to respond when the user double-clicks on an object in the FileSystemTree. If this object is a directory, this function will open it. If the object is not a directory, then another function, named logFileDetails, is called.

```
public function getDetails():void
{
    var node:File = tree.selectedItem as File;
    if(node != null)
    {
        if(!node.isDirectory)
        {
        logFileDetails(node);
        }

    }
}
```

Figure 12-11. The getDetails function

The logFileDetails function (Figure 12-12) takes the file that the user has double-clicked and figures out what to do with it. This first step is to separate the extension from the rest of the file. This is placed into the variable type. A switch then decides what to do based on the extension stored in type. The first three possibilities (png, jpg, and gif) are all image formats. Therefore, when a file with any of these extensions is selected, a function called showImage is called. We will build this function in a moment. To help the user see what is happening, we set a Text component to provide a message about the kind of media it is (Current Media is Image - .png, for example). In the same way, when an MP3 or FLV video is selected, we call the appropriate function (playSound or playVideo, respectively).

```
public function logFileDetails(file:File):void
{
    var type:String;
    type = (file.url.substr(file.url.lastIndexOf(".")));

    //Causes control to transfer to one of several statements,
    //depending on the value of an expression.
    switch (type)
    {
        case ".png":
            showImage(file.url);
            currentMediaType.text = "Current Media is Image  -   " + type;
        break;

        case ".jpg":
            showImage(file.url);
            currentMediaType.text = "Current Media is Image  -   " + type;
        break;

        case ".gif":
            showImage(file.url);
            currentMediaType.text = "Current Media is Image  -   " + type;
        break;

        case ".mp3":
            playSound(file.url);
            currentMediaType.text = "Current Media is Audio  -   " + type;
        break;

        case ".flv":
            playVideo(file.url);
            currentMediaType.text = "Current Media is Video  -   " + type;
        break;

        default:
        currentMediaType.text = "Current Media is not recognized  -   " + type;
    }
}
```

Figure 12-12. The logFileDetails function

To control the sound, we first create a sound channel. When the user double-clicks an MP3, the createSound function is called. This function creates a sound object and plays it through the sound channel. When the sound needs to be stopped, the stopSound function is called (Figure 12-13).

```
/*
The SoundChannel class controls a sound in an application. Each sound playing in an
Adobe® Flash® application is assigned to a sound channel, and the application can have
multiple sound channels that are mixed together. The SoundChannel class contains a stop()
method, properties for monitoring the amplitude (volume) of the channel, and a property
for setting a SoundTransform object to the channel.
*/
private var _channel:SoundChannel = new SoundChannel();

//
public function playSound (soundPath:String):void
{
    //If there is an audio file playing already, stop it.
    stopSound();
    //We need a variable of type to store the audio files
    var _sound:Sound = new Sound();
    _sound.load(new URLRequest(soundPath));
    //play sound file
    _channel = _sound.play();
}

//
private function stopSound():void{
    _channel.stop();
}
```

Figure 12-13. Functions that control sound

The functions for playing an image or a video are shown in Figure 12-14.

```
private function showImage(imgPath:String):void
{
    //stop sound
    stopSound();
    //hide video if playing
    display_vid.visible = false;
    display_vid.stop();
    display_img.load(imgPath);
}

//
private function playVideo(videoPath:String):void
{
    //stop sound
    stopSound();
    display_vid.visible = true;
    display_vid.source = videoPath;
}
    ]]>
</mx:Script>
```

Figure 12-14. Functions that display images and video

In the case of an image, sound is stopped (in case an MP3 was playing before this image was selected), the video display is made invisible and stopped (in case a video was playing before), and the image is loaded. In the case of a video, sound is stopped in case a sound file was playing, the video display is made visible, and the video is loaded.

9. If you are not using the MediaCenter-start file, add the ActionScript shown in Figures 12-9 to 12-14 now.

You will notice that you get a series of error messages when you first put this code in. This is because our functions are often set to perform actions on components that we have not yet created.

Connecting FileSystemTree to functions

You can connect the FileSystemTree to the functions by either adding the code directly to the MXML tag in the Source view or by adding the names of the functions to the properties of the component in the Design view.

10. In the Design view, select the FileSystemTree. Switch to the Category View of the Properties panel and open the Events folder. This folder allows you to call a function that you created in ActionScript for any of the possible events for that component. In this case, we add initTree() for the creationComplete event (this will run the function that we created that points our component to the desktop as soon as the component is created) and getDetails() for the doubleClick event. The getDetails function looks at what the user double-clicked and initiates the appropriate function (showImage, playSound, or playVideo). This is shown in Figure 12-15.

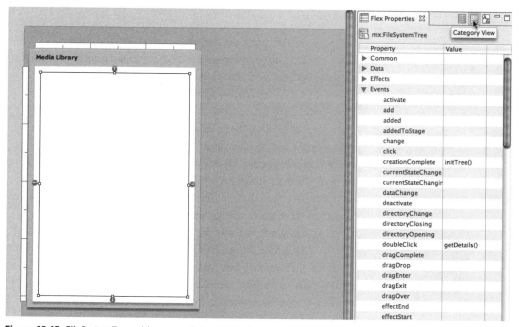

Figure 12-15. FileSystemTree with events that call functions

If you look back at this component in the Source view, you can see how the tag has been changed (Figure 12-16). You can add this code manually if you find it easier.

```
<mx:FileSystemTree left="10" right="10" top="10" bottom="10" creationComplete="initTree()" doubleClick="getDetails()"/>
```

Figure 12-16. MXML tag for FileSystemTree

247

Adding the remaining components

We have now created the FileSystemTree and the code that goes with it. Next let's create the components that respond to the FileSystemTree. Specifically this will be the display area for the media and a Text component to show our message about the media.

11. Drag an Image component next to the Panel. This component will display our images and has an ID of display_img. Set the Layout constraints as shown in Figure 12-17.

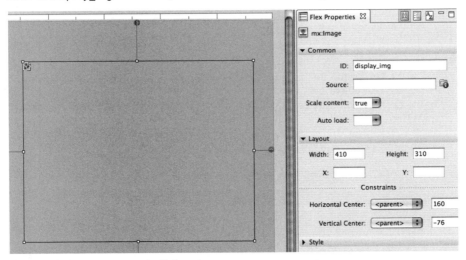

Figure 12-17. Image component with layout

12. Drag a VideoDisplay component out and place it in the same area as the image component. Scale it until it is approximately the correct size (Figure 12-18). If you are concerned with getting the best video image, the size of the video display should be a multiple of the size of the original video. The ID for the VideoDisplay is display_vid.

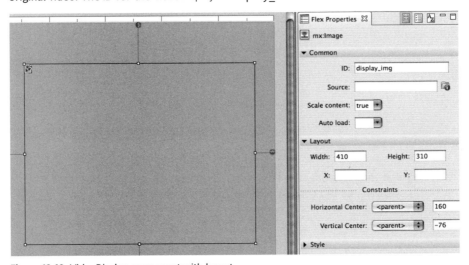

Figure 12-18. VideoDisplay component with layout

13. In the Category view of the Properties panel, set autoPlay to true and visible to false. This means that the video won't be visible until we make it visible in our function (Figure 12-19).

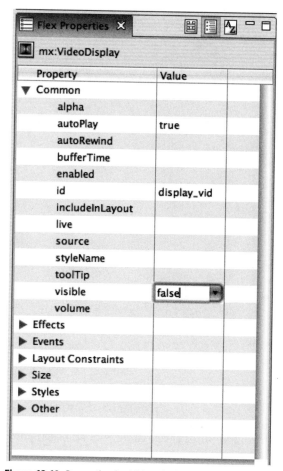

Figure 12-19. Properties for VideoDisplay component

14. Add a Text component below the image display. This component will tell us what kind of media is currently selected. The ID for the component is currentMediaType and the Text property is Current Media is: (Figure 12-20).

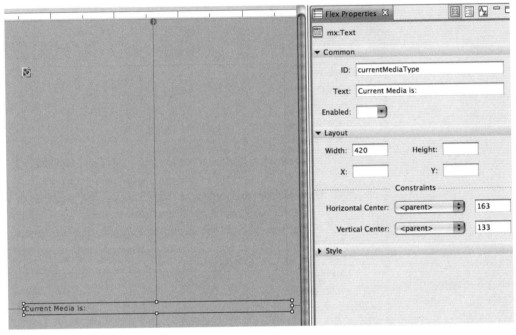

Figure 12-20. Text component that displays the file type

15. Run the project.

Running the project will show you the current project. The shortcut keys are the same for running an AIR application as before: Shift+Ctrl+F11 (Windows)/Shift+Cmd+F11 (Mac). Notice that the project did not open in a browser as our previous Flex projects have. Instead, it opens in a program called AIR Debug Launcher (ADL).

When you select an image from the FileSystemTree, it will appear in the display area, as shown in Figure 12-21.

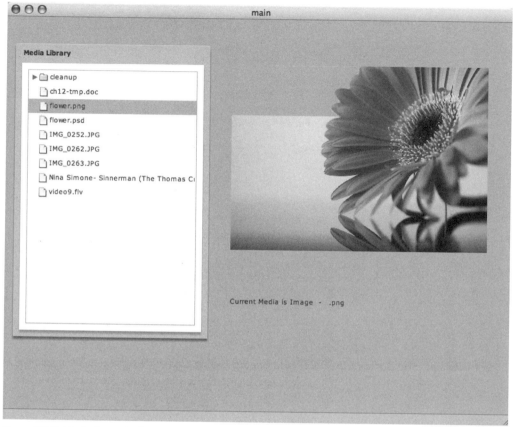

Figure 12-21. Media Center before CSS styling

Adding CSS

Adding CSS to an AIR application is done the same way as we have done in previous Flex projects. If you use the Flex Style Explorer to change the CSS style for the application background, the CSS must refer to WindowedApplication, not Application. This is because an AIR application uses a WindowedApplication as opposed to an Application by default. You need to manually change this in the CSS file if you are using the Style Explorer. The CSS file used to style this project is shown in Figure 12-22.

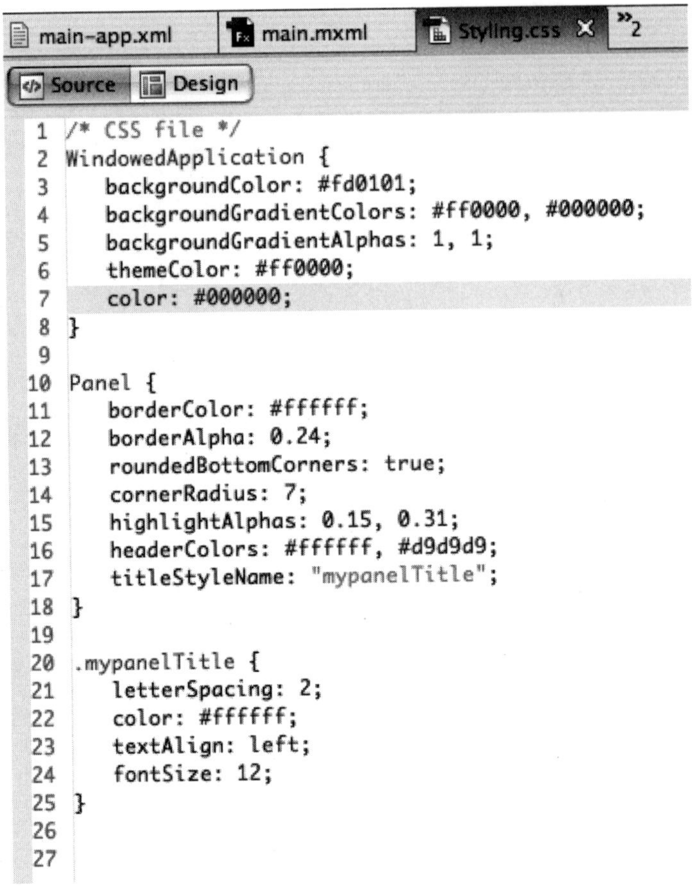

```
main–app.xml        main.mxml        Styling.css  ✕   »2

</> Source    Design

 1  /* CSS file */
 2  WindowedApplication {
 3      backgroundColor: #fd0101;
 4      backgroundGradientColors: #ff0000, #000000;
 5      backgroundGradientAlphas: 1, 1;
 6      themeColor: #ff0000;
 7      color: #000000;
 8  }
 9
10  Panel {
11      borderColor: #ffffff;
12      borderAlpha: 0.24;
13      roundedBottomCorners: true;
14      cornerRadius: 7;
15      highlightAlphas: 0.15, 0.31;
16      headerColors: #ffffff, #d9d9d9;
17      titleStyleName: "mypanelTitle";
18  }
19
20  .mypanelTitle {
21      letterSpacing: 2;
22      color: #ffffff;
23      textAlign: left;
24      fontSize: 12;
25  }
26
27
```

Figure 12-22. CSS styling

Figure 12-23 shows how we styled this project. This version of the project is available as Media-Center-Stage1Complete.zip in the download for this chapter.

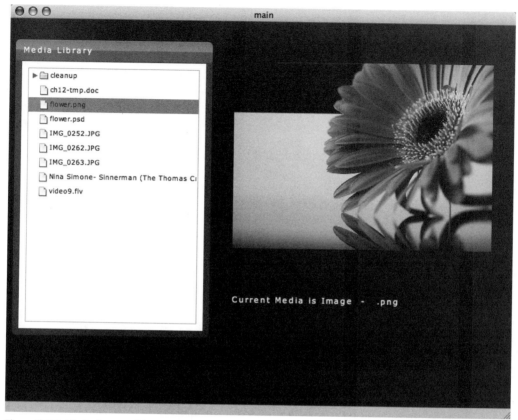

Figure 12-23. Media Center with CSS styling

Exporting an AIR package

Instead of being shown in a browser, AIR applications are programs that are installed onto the user's computer.

16. To create this installation file, select Project ➤ Export Release Version (Figure 12-24).

Figure 12-24. Export command for AIR Applications

17. This brings up the Export Release Version dialog box (Figure 12-25). Here you set the project and MXML file that you wish to export. Specify the location and name of the file that you want to create in the Export to file field and click Next. It is good form to include the extension (.air) when naming your file.

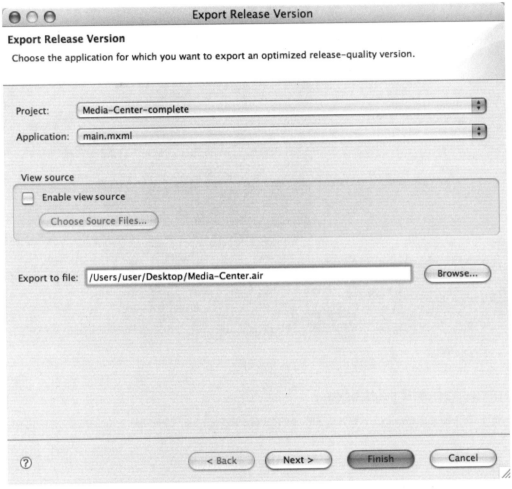

Figure 12-25. Exporting the AIR application

This brings us to the digital signature page. All AIR applications must have a digital signature before they can be distributed to other computers. These indicate to the user where the program is coming from and prevents users from accidentally or maliciously re-creating your application. You can either get a certificate from certificates authorities (CAs) such as VeriSign or Thawte or you can self-sign. Having a certificate from a CA gives users a greater sense of confidence when installing new software on their machine. To keep things simple, we will self-sign.

18. To self-sign an application, select Export and sign an AIR file with a digital certificate, and click Create (Figure 12-26).

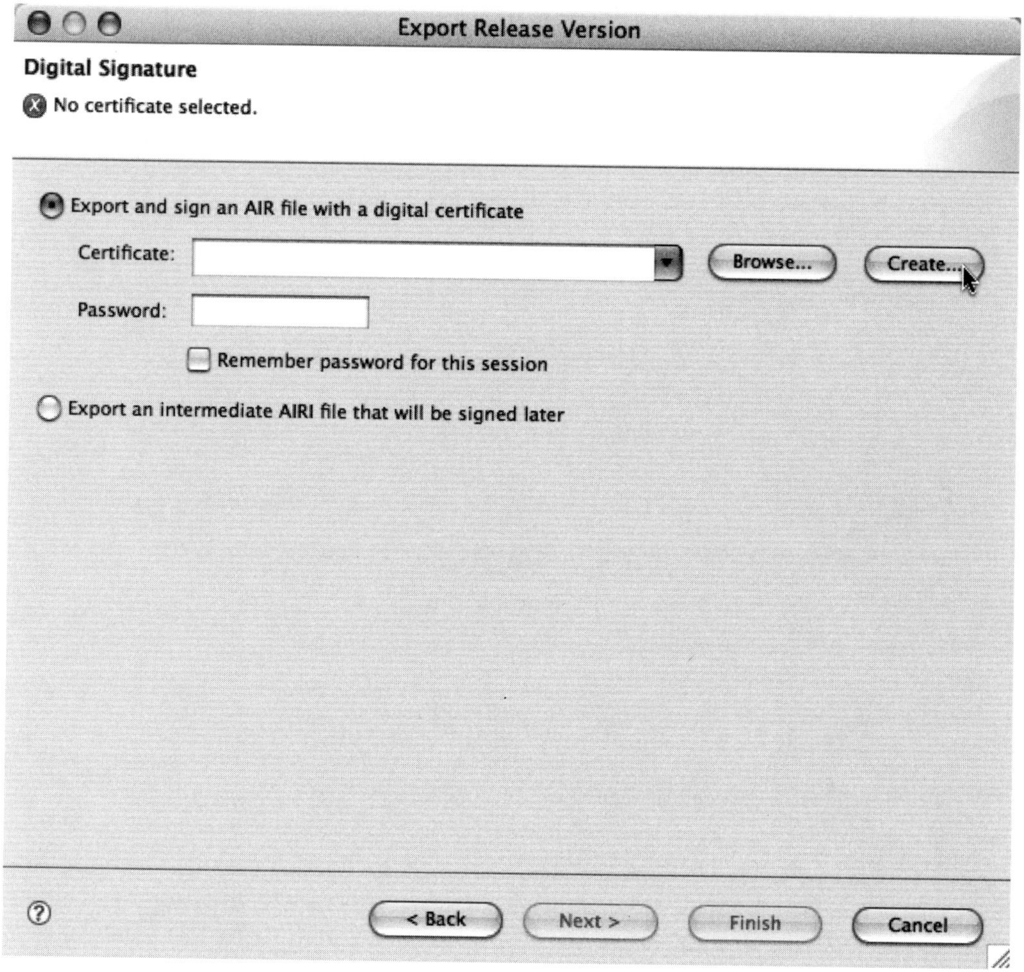

Figure 12-26. Digital Signature page

19. Fill out the form for the certificate and click OK. This information will be shown to users when they install the application (Figure 12-27).

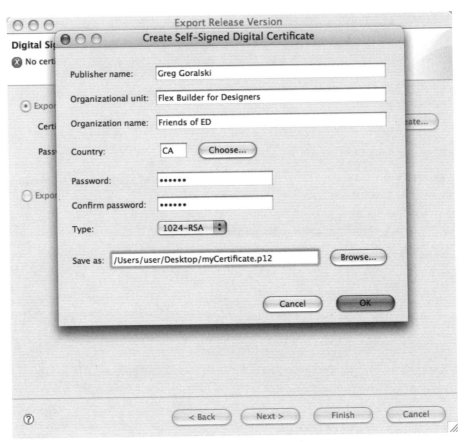

Figure 12-27. Certificate information for the AIR application certificate

20. Click Finish.

Double-clicking on the file that has been created (named Media-Center.air) starts the installer, which guides you through the process of adding it to your computer. It is this .air file that is distributed to the users.

Controlling the application window

A very interesting feature of AIR applications is the ability to control the window in which they are presented. In this section, we will remove the default rectangle window of the application and give it a custom look, establishing an image to be our background and shape of our application.

Figure 12-28 shows a version of our Media Center that has had the rectangular window replaced with a background image that is partially transparent. By making the background image partially transparent, you can create any shape for your application that you wish.

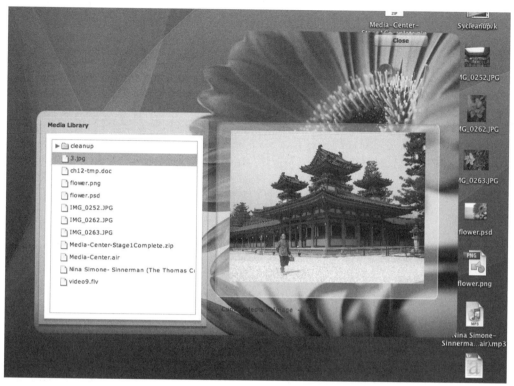

Figure 12-28. Media Center with custom background

Getting rid of the box

We remove the window around the application by modifying the MXML, the CSS, and the settings in the application descriptor file (the main-app.xml file that was created automatically when we started the project).

When we first created the AIR project, Flex Builder put in the WindowedApplication MXML tag automatically (Figure 12-29).

```
1  <?xml version="1.0" encoding="utf-8"?>
2  <mx:WindowedApplication xmlns:mx="http://www.adobe.com/2006/mxml" layout="absolute">
3
4  </mx:WindowedApplication>
5
```

Figure 12-29. Default application tag for an AIR project

1. Change this tag from WindowedApplication to Application. Remember to do this for the start and the end of the tag.

The next step involves taking a close look at the application descriptor file. This file controls the way that the final application is seen and installed. It is an XML file that gives you parameters to control the name of the application, along with other information such as description and copyright information. The part of the file that we are going to look into in detail contains the window attributes. Figure 12-30 shows the default settings.

```
44
45    <!--
46        The main content file of the application, which must be a SWF or
47        HTML file. (Required.)
48
49        Attributes:
50        systemChrome - "standard" or "none". If "standard", the application
51                        window is opened with operating system-specific window
52                        elements such as a title bar, minimize, and close
53                        buttons. If "none", the application must provide its
54                        own window controls. (Note, the Flex WindowedApplication
55                        class supplies a set of window controls, which are only
56                        shown when systemChrome="none".)
57        transparent  - "true" or "false". If "true", the application has support
58                        for full transparency.
59        visible      - "true" or "false". If "false", the main window will not
60                        be displayed
61                        until the application changes the window visible property
62                        to "true".
63        width        - the initial window height (including chrome).
64        height       - the initial window width (including chrome).
65
66        In Flex Builder, the SWF reference required within this tag will be set
67        automatically when you launch or export this application.
68    -->
69    <rootContent systemChrome="standard" transparent="false" visible="true">[SWF reference is generated]</rootContent>
70
```

Figure 12-30. Application descriptor file

In Figure 12-30, you can see that we can set five attributes for the window. Most of this text consists of comments to explain the options and it is only the last line (starting with <rootContent) that is read by the computer. We will be changing the first two of the attributes.

2. Set the systemChrome attribute to none. This will remove the operating system window.

3. Set the transparent setting to true. This will allow the background to be transparent once we remove the background color.

We get rid of any background color in our application through the CSS attributes.

4. Replace the CSS with that shown in Figure 12-31.

Figure 12-31. CSS that removes the background

The CSS simply makes the background of the application transparent.

This leaves our components floating in space—generally not a great look. Let's fix this by adding an image to serve as the shape and background of the application. To make the application shape non-rectangular, the image that you use must have some transparent areas. The image used in this example is called background.png (Figure 12-32). You can use the graphics program of your choice to create this image.

Figure 12-32. Image for our custom background

5. Drag an Image component onto your project. For ID type background and for source type background.png.

This has now given us a nonrectangular application. But the loss of the window has also taken away some of the functionality we need for our application. Specifically, the ability to move an application around your screen and the ability to close an application are controlled through the window.

We can re-create this functionality in our application.

Re-creating the functionality

Let's start with the ability to close an application. We do this by importing the close event and creating a function to run the event. Use the code shown in Figure 12-33.

```
import mx.events.CloseEvent;

public function close():void {
    stage.window.close();
}
```

Figure 12-33. ActionScript that allows the window to be closed

6. Add the `import` command after the previous `import` commands close to the start of the `<mx:script>` tag. Add the close function to the end of the other functions that exist in the project. Remember that all ActionScript must be placed within the `<mx:Script></mx:Script>` tags.

7. Add a button to run this code. The button uses the `OnClick` event to call the function `close()`, as shown in Figure 12-34.

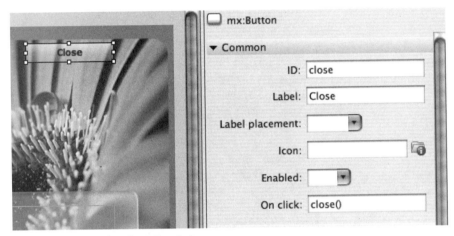

Figure 12-34. Button that closes the window

Adding the drag functionality

The ability to drag the application through the background image is also created by a function. The code is shown in Figure 12-35.

```
// drag Application as background image is dragged
public function initAppDrag():void {
    backgroundImage.addEventListener( MouseEvent.MOUSE_DOWN, startMove );
}
public function startMove(event:MouseEvent):void {
    stage.window.startMove();
}
```

Figure 12-35. Functions that allow the application to be dragged

As you can see, this code consists of two functions. The first creates a listener so that we know when the mouse is clicked on the background image. The second changes the position of the window based on the mouse movements.

8. Add this code at the bottom of the previous functions within the <mx:Script> tags.

Since a function always needs to be called by something, we call the initAppDrag function when the background image is first loaded in. We trigger the initAppDrag function through a creationComplete event. It is simplest to add this directly to the image MXML tag in the Source view. Add the creationComplete event to the Image component by adding creationComplete="initAppDrag()", as shown in Figure 12-36.

```
<mx:Image x="3" y="10" width="796" height="580" id="backgroundImage" source="background.png" creationComplete="initAppDrag()"
```

Figure 12-36. Image MXML tag with dragging initiation event

Summary

As you learned in this chapter, using Flex Builder to create AIR applications opens a lot of new opportunities. With AIR you create applications that are not accessed through the Internet but that are installed on users' computer. This allows applications to continue functioning even when no Internet access is available. These applications still have the ability to access the Internet and load data when the computer is connected.

You can also create applications that have easy access to the hard drive of the user. The example that we created also used the ability of AIR applications to create a distinct application window shape that used the alpha channel to hide part of the background image.

Congratulations on making it through the book. You now have a diverse set of tools to control the look and feel of a Rich Internet Application, you can create applications for both the Web and the desktop, and you can use the built-in features of Flex Builder, such as fluid layout and drag-and-drop. We wish you all the best in your adventures with Flex.

INDEX

1-59059-543-2 $39.99 [US]

1-59059-518-1 $39.99 [US]

1-59059-542-4 $36.99 [US]

1-59059-517-3 $39.99 [US]

1-59059-651-X $44.99 [US]

EXPERIENCE THE DESIGNER TO DESIGNER™ DIFFERENCE

1-59059-558-0 $49.99 [US]

1-59059-314-6 $59.99 [US]

1-59059-315-4 $59.99 [US]

1-59059-619-6 $44.99 [US]

1-59059-304-9 $49.99 [US]

1-59059-355-3 $24.99 [US]

1-59059-409-6 $39.99 [US]

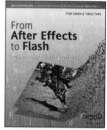

1-59059-748-6 $49.99 [US]

1-59059-593-9 $49.99 [US]

1-59059-555-6 $44.99 [US]

1-59059-533-5 $34.99 [US]

1-59059-638-2 $49.99 [US]

1-59059-765-6 $34.99 [US]

1-59059-581-5 $39.99 [US]

1-59059-614-5 $34.99 [US]

1-59059-594-7 $39.99 [US]

1-59059-381-2 $34.99 [US]

1-59059-554-8 $24.99 [US]

friendsofed.com/forums

Join the friends of ED forums to find out more about our books, discover useful technology tips and tricks, or get a helping hand on a challenging project. *Designer to Designer*™ is what it's all about—our community sharing ideas and inspiring each other. In the friends of ED forums, you'll find a wide range of topics to discuss, so look around, find a forum, and dive right in!

- **Books and Information**

  Chat about friends of ED books, gossip about the community, or even tell us some bad jokes!

- **Flash**

  Discuss design issues, ActionScript, dynamic content, and video and sound.

- **Web Design**

  From front-end frustrations to back-end blight, share your problems and your knowledge here.

- **Site Check**

  Show off your work or get new ideas.

- **Digital Imagery**

  Create eye candy with Photoshop, Fireworks, Illustrator, and FreeHand.

- **ArchivED**

  Browse through an archive of old questions and answers.

HOW TO PARTICIPATE

Go to the friends of ED forums at **www.friendsofed.com/forums**.

Visit **www.friendsofed.com** to get the latest on our books, find out what's going on in the community, and discover some of the slickest sites online today!

friendsof ED™
DESIGNER TO DESIGNER™
an Apress® company